From Broke & Broken to BornAgain Bo$$ Babe

PinkPrint
to
Perseverance

Tara Hirshberg

ISBN: 978-1-969463-65-5

Table of Contents

INTRODUCTION

Pour Yourself a Pink Pitcher of Lemonade

Welcome, unstoppable woman!

If you're holding this book, it means you're ready for a new season—a season of strength, grace, and unstoppable growth. You're here because, like me, you've been handed a few lemons in life. But, instead of letting them sour your spirit, you're determined to squeeze every last drop of wisdom from them and turn them into the sweetest pitcher of pink lemonade this world has ever seen.

This isn't just another self-help book. This is your PinkPrint—a feminine, faith-filled roadmap to perseverance, pivoting, and finding purpose even in the messiest seasons. It's a love letter to the woman who's been knocked down and decided to rise up stronger.

Why PinkPrint?

You might be wondering why I call it a PinkPrint instead of just a blueprint like everyone else. A blueprint is usually something technical and structured, like an architect's plan for building a house or a bridge. It's precise, detailed, and straightforward. While that's great for construction, life—especially a woman's life—often needs a little more heart, soul, and faith.

That's where the PinkPrint comes in. It's not just about plans and structures. It's about bringing your whole self into the journey.

What Makes It Pink?

The PinkPrint is pink because it embraces the beauty and grace of femininity. It celebrates our unique strengths as women—our compassion, resilience, creativity, and unstoppable spirit. It honors the way we nurture, lead, and create impact in the world.

What Makes It a Print?

It's called a print because it's a plan, a guide, a roadmap to help you design a life that aligns with your dreams and values. Just like an architect's blueprint provides structure and guidance for building something extraordinary, your PinkPrint gives you the steps to build the extraordinary life God has planned for you.

What Makes It Faith-Filled?

Unlike a traditional blueprint, the PinkPrint is rooted in faith. True success doesn't come from just ticking boxes. It comes from trusting God's purpose for us, listening to His whispers, and letting the Holy Spirit guide your steps. When you combine practical steps with divine wisdom, you create a life that's not only successful, but deeply meaningful.

What You'll Find in These Pages

In these pages, you'll find my story—the journey from a broke and broken woman to the Born Again Bo$$Babe I am today. You'll read about the tears, the prayers, the sleepless nights, and the spark of faith that never went out, even when the world tried to blow it out.

But this book isn't just about me. It's about you.

Every chapter is designed to help you discover your own unstoppable strength. You'll learn how to build a life and a business that align with your faith, and how to embrace the woman God created you to be. I've woven in lessons from my journey, along with practical steps, reflection questions, and powerful strategies that you can put into action today.

You'll discover how to turn setbacks into setups, how to pivot with grace, and why faith is more than just a foundation. It's the cherry on top of your success sundae. You'll learn how to design your own lemonade stand by building multiple income streams, and you'll unlock the signature PinkPrint system that has guided me and so many others through seasons of growth and change.

A Movement of Unstoppable Women

This PinkPrint is more than just a book. It's a movement. It's a sisterhood of women who refuse to settle for the status quo. Women who choose faith over fear, progress over perfection, and community over comparison.

So grab your pen, open your heart, and pour yourself a big, sweet pitcher of pink lemonade. Let's begin this journey together. Your PinkPrint to Perseverance is waiting for you, one step, one pivot, and one prayer at a time.

CHAPTER 1

When Life Hands You Lemons — A Little Girl with Big Lemons

Opening Story: Setting the Scene

I was born in 1983 to a teenage mom who was just nineteen years old. My parents were high school sweethearts, full of dreams and possibilities, but also carrying the weight of growing up too fast themselves. I was the first child in the family, a little girl who had no idea just how quickly life would hand her a pitcher of lemons.

My sister, Heather, came along two years later. My parents' marriage couldn't hold together under the pressures of young adulthood. And when I was just three years old, it ended in divorce.

The memory that stands out most is being woken up and told that we were leaving Florida to move to Michigan with my Aunt Verda. I felt like I was being swept away from everything I knew, even though I didn't fully understand why.

Growing up as the eldest child meant stepping into the role of being the responsible one. I was expected to be the perfect, obedient child. My family would tell you that I took charge from a very young age, always being the "good girl." Rarely, if ever, did I get into trouble. I was a rule-follower by nature, groomed to listen and do what was right, as well as keep the peace even when everything around me felt uncertain.

Looking back, I can see how those early experiences planted the seeds of resilience, even if I didn't realize it at the time. They taught me how to step up, carry responsibility, and be the glue that held things together when life got messy. Little did I know that those lessons would become the foundation of my *PinkPrint to Perseverance*—the map I would follow, again and again, as I faced even bigger challenges later in life.

Becoming the Second Mom

Now, being part of a single-mother household, I was instantly transformed into the second mom. My mom was determined to build a better future for us, working hard to get through nursing school. She spent long days and even longer nights studying, working, and doing everything she could to make ends meet.

At just a young age, I stepped up to help her keep things running smoothly. I became the extra set of hands and the pair of eyes watching over my sister. It wasn't just babysitting after school—it was making sure homework was done, dinners were made, and we had everything we needed to make it through the day.

I would help my sister get ready for bed and watch over her at night. Mornings came early, and I would do my best to manage my own schoolwork and responsibilities, even when it felt like the weight of the world was on my small shoulders.

I learned quickly that resilience wasn't just about being strong; it was about finding a way to keep going when everything felt heavy. Sacrifices became second nature: giving up time with friends, skipping activities that other kids took for granted, and carrying the emotional load of a family trying to build a new life.

Looking back, I can see how those nights watching over Heather and those days, running a household alongside my mom, were building me into the woman I am today. Every responsibility, every sacrifice, and every challenge taught me that when life hands you lemons, you learn how to squeeze them into something sweet—no matter how tired you might be.

Growing Up Fast

Being an instant mom forced me to grow up quickly. I didn't get to ease into adulthood like some kids do. Instead, I was handed a heavy dose of responsibility early on, and it left its mark on me. I had to learn to be strong when others needed me, to put their needs before my own, and to make decisions that sometimes felt too big for my young heart.

This responsibility taught me to take the more mature path in every situation. I couldn't afford to be reckless or carefree. I learned to weigh my choices carefully, to consider how my actions would affect my sister and my mom.

Those experiences didn't just shape my sense of responsibility; they built my resilience. Every challenge and every moment that I felt like the adult in the room taught me perseverance. I learned how to pivot quickly when plans changed or obstacles came my way.

Growing up even faster happened at age fourteen, when my mom had her 3rd girl. My mom likes to joke that she had her babysitters first, then she had her baby. At fourteen, I was an instant mom all over again. This time, I was in high school, spending my nights changing diapers, bottle-feeding, and giving breathing treatments to a very fussy newborn. My mom worked nights so she could be home during the day with my baby sister, so from seven at night until seven in the morning, I was mom to both my sisters. Then I'd get up and go to high school. Talk about the best form of birth control ever. Let's just say it gave me a whole new appreciation for how much work goes into caring for a newborn.

Looking back, I see how these moments formed the backbone of my independence and my work ethic. They taught me that even when the world feels like it's falling apart, I have the strength to hold it all together. Those early lessons were the seeds that helped me grow into the woman I am today, ready to take on whatever life throws my way.

Silver Linings in the Struggle

Even in the midst of all these struggles, I can see the silver linings now. Being the second mom in the household meant I had to grow up quickly, but that quick maturity became a gift in its own way. I didn't have the time or the desire to fall into trouble like so many teenagers did. I didn't experiment with drugs or alcohol, and I never felt drawn to risky behaviors. There was simply too much on my plate, too many responsibilities, to even think about going down the wrong path.

That sense of responsibility gave me a clear direction that kept me out of the messes that can derail young people. It wasn't always easy, but it taught me discipline and focus that I carried into adulthood. I learned to find purpose in every task, no matter how small, and to take pride in being the steady hand in our household.

Looking back, I can see that my relationship with Heather was shaped by the role I played in her life. Because I was more like a second mom than a sister, we didn't always get along. She often saw me as the authority figure rather than the big sister she could confide in. It wasn't until we grew up that we were able to set aside those old roles and finally build the sisterly bond we both longed for.

Those tough times built a foundation of resilience I didn't fully understand until much later. They taught me that strength is forged in the fires of responsibility, and that even when life felt overwhelming, I could adapt and keep moving forward. Those were the earliest building blocks of the PinkPrint that would guide me through every challenge to come.

The Birth of Problem-Solving Over Panic

Problem-solving over panic became my superpower. My life was, in many ways, organized chaos—a constant cycle of challenges that could have easily overwhelmed me. But instead of letting each problem become a roadblock, I chose to see every challenge as an opportunity to grow.

This mindset gave me the resilience and peace of mind to handle tough situations with grace. Whenever life threw me a curveball, my first instinct wasn't to panic. Instead, I would take a deep breath, stay calm, and come up with an effective solution. I learned that no matter what the problem was, there was always a way to figure it out. Giving up was never an option.

I still remember one of my first big lessons in problem-solving: I was seventeen when I decided to buy my first car at a local auction. It was a beautiful black sports car, rolling through the auction line with the engine purring. No one was bidding, and at seventeen, I thought I was getting the deal of a lifetime when I won that car for $500. I was so excited.

But that excitement quickly faded when I realized the car had one big issue—it didn't have a working reverse gear. It would drive forward just fine, but when I put it in reverse, it wouldn't budge. I went to the auctioneer, explaining the problem, only to be reminded that all cars at auction are sold as is. No one else was bidding because, apparently, the car guys knew it had this issue.

At seventeen, with my hard-earned money invested, I faced a choice: panic or problem-solve. And I chose to problem-solve.

For almost a year, I drove that car without a reverse gear. I learned to strategically park so I could always pull through a spot or circle a section if I needed to go backward. I made it work until I could afford to buy another car.

That experience taught me that there's always a way to make something work. Every challenge is an invitation to get creative, keep moving forward, and trust that there's a solution waiting to be found.

Problem-solving over panic became my signature move—a mindset that would guide me through every pivot in my journey. It was the backbone of my perseverance, reminding me that when life hands you lemons, you don't panic. You find a way to make the sweetest pink lemonade anyone has ever tasted.

Reflection: The Lessons That Built Me

When I look back on those early years, I can see how every challenge, every late night, and every sacrifice planted seeds that grew into the woman I am today.

Those experiences taught me independence—to stand on my own two feet, make decisions that mattered, and carry the weight of responsibility even when it felt heavy. I didn't wait for someone else to solve my problems. I became the girl who took charge, who did what needed to be done, no matter how hard it seemed.

They also taught me resilience. Every time life knocked me down, I got back up stronger. I learned that no matter how tough things got, I could keep going. Resilience became my secret weapon, the silent strength that carried me through the storms.

I also gained the power of perspective. I saw firsthand that challenges weren't the end of the story. They were stepping stones, lessons, and even blessings in disguise. When you've faced enough problems and learned to rise above them, you start to see every obstacle as an opportunity to grow.

And perhaps, most importantly, I developed resourcefulness. With limited resources and plenty of challenges, I learned to be creative, think outside the box, and find a way to make things work. Whether it was managing a household, driving a car without reverse, or juggling schoolwork and family responsibilities, I found a way.

All of these lessons planted the seeds of the woman I would become. They built a foundation of strength, faith, and determination that would guide me through every pivot in my journey. They shaped my PinkPrint—the blueprint for how to turn life's lemons into pink lemonade—and they remind me every day that I was made for this.

A Look Ahead: What's Next

The lessons I learned during those early years—independence, resilience, perspective, and resourcefulness—became the first building blocks of my PinkPrint. They gave me the strength to stand tall in the face of challenges, and the wisdom to pivot when life demanded it.

As we move into the next chapter, I invite you to come with me as I show you how these lessons helped me navigate even bigger challenges. Together, we'll explore how to face adversity with faith and turn every obstacle into an opportunity for growth.

Reflection Questions

- Which challenges during your childhood or early life shaped your strength?
- When did you learn to solve problems instead of panicking?
- Who or what in your life taught you the most about perseverance?
- Think back to a time when you had to step up before you were ready. How did that moment shape your character?
- Describe a moment from your childhood when you felt proud of your resilience.
- List three small ways you can practice problem-solving over panic in your life today.

CHAPTER 2

Breaking Barriers — Facing Challenges Head On

Chapter Overview

In this chapter, I'm taking you into the raw and honest parts of my adult life where I faced some of my biggest barriers yet—marriage struggles, divorce, corporate layoffs, and the journey from feeling broken to becoming the Born Again Bo$$Babe you know today. I want you to see firsthand how the lessons I learned in my early years (the ones we talked about in Chapter 1) became my lifeline in the storms that hit me later.

This isn't just a story of falling apart. It's about what it looks like to pick yourself up with faith, resilience, and an unshakable belief that God's got something better waiting on the other side. So grab a cup of coffee, get comfy, and let's dive into this season together—because it's here, in the middle of the mess, that I discovered the PinkPrint that changed everything.

Introduction: When the American Dream Turns Sour

Breaking barriers isn't just about pushing through external obstacles—it's about confronting the deeply personal struggles that can derail even the strongest among us. For me, those barriers came in the form of a crumbling marriage, a toxic corporate career, and a life that looked perfect on the outside but was suffocating on the inside.

When life knocked me down, I had a choice: stay broken or become unbreakable. I chose to trust God, pivot, and build the life I was truly meant to live.

The resilience, perseverance, and problem-solving superpower I developed in my childhood were about to be tested like never before. Everything I had learned about making lemonade from lemons would be put into action as my world turned upside down.

Setting the Stage

In 2011, life seemed to be falling perfectly into place. I was living what many would call the American Dream. After years of cold Michigan winters, I finally packed up my life and moved to sunny Florida—a dream I'd always had. My Corporate America career gave me the opportunity to transfer from Grand Rapids, Michigan to Bradenton, Florida, and I seized it without hesitation.

My fiancé and soon-to-be husband came along for the ride. We got married, bought a beautiful pool home, and both of us had good-paying careers. From the outside, it looked like we had it all. The American Dream—warm weather, a lovely home, a good salary, and a promising career—everything I thought I'd ever wanted.

But dreams don't always look the same on the inside.

Within six years, that dream had soured. By 2017, at the age of thirty-four, my carefully constructed life crumbled. In the span of just one year, I found myself divorced, laid off from my 12-year Corporate America career, and over a thousand miles away from my family.

I had always clung to some powerful truths that guided me through challenges:

"You were designed by God for greatness and a purpose."
"Work around your life—don't live around your work."
"Time is your most valuable resource—don't waste it."

At the age of thirty-four, in a season of profound change, I found myself holding onto these mottos like a lifeline. While most people would have crumbled, I chose to see it as a sign from God to completely reinvent my life and finally live with purpose and freedom.

Divorced to Dreaming Again — My Story

Let's rewind three years prior to that turning point.

From the outside, everyone would have thought my life was picture-perfect. I had moved from cold Michigan to sunny Florida, gotten married, bought a large pool home, and secured a well-paying job in Corporate America. I was ticking all the boxes society says you're supposed to tick.

But on the inside, that American Dream was stealing my joy, draining my energy, and suffocating my sense of freedom. My marriage was built on broken trust—an unfaithful man who was also married to his work. That large pool home felt more like a prison than a sanctuary. I found every excuse I could to be anywhere but inside those walls.

My career, though something I was good at, devoured all of my precious time. I wasn't living the life I had imagined, and deep down, I knew something had to change.

Then, one Sunday, everything shifted. During an impromptu Holy Spirit nudge at church, I found myself crying and walking straight to the baptistery in my full clothes—jeans and all. That moment of surrender was the catalyst for an avalanche of transformation. I gave it all to God. I had been living for myself and the American Dream, but I knew there was so much more to life.

Shortly after that, my husband asked for a divorce. I sold that large pool home and downsized into a maintenance-free condo that fit my new season. A few months later, I was laid off and downsized out of my Corporate America career of twelve years. It felt like my life was falling apart. But in reality, it was all falling into place. God was removing the people, places, and things that weren't part of His plan for my future.

Emotionally, I was a wreck during that first year of change. But I clung to my faith that God had a plan, a purpose, and a reason for it all. To hold everything together, I found an incredible support group of women and an awesome church community. Faith and community became my anchors in a sea of uncertainty.

Through faith, I found my sparkle again and completely reinvented myself—this time in God's way. I wanted to live differently and wouldn't settle for the ordinary when extraordinary was within me. I wanted to be an example to other divorced women, showing them that hope exists, and a new path to success is always possible.

A Look Back: Lessons from the Pivotal Year

This season of my life was the ultimate test of my resilience and faith. It taught me that:

- Brokenness is often the soil where breakthroughs grow.
- When life falls apart, it's often God making space for something better.
- The barriers we face—broken marriages, job loss, betrayal—can either bury us or build us.

Through this season, I discovered the essence of my PinkPrint to perseverance:

- Faith Over Fear: Trusting God's plan even when everything is falling apart.
- Problem-Solving Over Panic: Choosing to pivot instead of giving up.
- Community Over Isolation: Leaning on faith-filled support systems.

These lessons became the backbone of my PinkPrint—the system I now share with other women who want to turn their lemons into the sweetest pink lemonade imaginable.

Reflection Questions

- What barriers in your life have felt impossible to overcome?
- How might God be using your brokenness to prepare you for breakthrough?
- Who can you lean on for support as you navigate these challenges?

A Look Ahead: Turning Barriers into Lemonade

In the next chapter, we'll explore how every obstacle is a hidden opportunity—and how to turn those lemons into a lemonade stand that's uniquely yours.

CHAPTER 3

The Power of Perseverance and Pivoting — Turning Setbacks into Setups

Chapter Overview

This chapter is all about the power of perseverance and the art of pivoting—how I turned life's biggest setbacks into setups for something greater. It builds on the resilience and problem-solving skills I developed in my early years, as well as the barriers I faced in adulthood. This is where I unpack the mindset shifts and practical lessons that taught me how to thrive, not just survive, when life didn't go as planned.

Learning from Obstacles

If there's one thing I've learned, it's that every obstacle in life comes with a hidden gift—a lesson that can either hold you back or help you grow. I chose to let my obstacles teach me strength and adaptability, to see them as classrooms rather than prisons.

One of the hardest lessons came from my marriage. I thought I had built the perfect life—marriage, home, career—but the foundation wasn't as solid as it appeared. When trust was broken, and I realized the dream wasn't what I'd hoped, I had to make the heartbreaking decision to walk away. It wasn't easy, but that obstacle taught me that sometimes letting go is the most courageous thing you can do.

In my career, I faced a layoff after twelve years of dedication and loyalty. I could have let that loss define me, but instead, I saw it as a redirection—a chance to finally build the life and business I'd always dreamed of. That layoff became the push I needed to step into my own calling.

Friendships, too, taught me valuable lessons. There were people I thought would always be in my life who turned out to be there for just a season. It hurt to let go, but each time I did, God brought someone better—someone who aligned with the woman I was becoming.

Looking back, I see how these obstacles were never the end of my story. They were stepping stones that taught me how to pivot, persevere, and trust that every setback was actually a setup for something greater.

If I had given up every time life threw me a curveball, I would have never discovered the woman I was meant to be. The difference between staying stuck and growing was learning to adapt—to find the lesson in loss and the opportunity in obstacles.

My early lessons in resilience—watching my mom work nights while I cared for my sisters, learning to be a second mom, and figuring out how to make things work when life felt chaotic—were the training ground for the challenges I faced as an adult. Those skills didn't just stay in childhood; they showed up every time I faced an obstacle as an adult.

Through every challenge, I learned that the only way to truly grow is to refuse to see the obstacle as a dead end. Instead, I started asking myself: What is this teaching me? How can I pivot? Where is God in this?

Each time, I found that the obstacle was actually a divine invitation to become more—more faithful, more adaptable, and more determined to live the life I was born to lead.

Pivotal Moments

Life has a way of presenting us with crossroads—moments that force us to make choices that ultimately shape who we become. These pivotal moments don't always come neatly packaged or arrive with a roadmap. But looking back, I see how each one was a nudge from God to trust Him more deeply and to let go of what no longer served me.

One of the most defining, pivotal moments was when I moved to Florida. I was trading cold Michigan winters for sunshine, but it wasn't just about the weather. It was about stepping out of my comfort zone and saying *yes* to a new life, even when it meant leaving behind familiar faces and routines. That move taught me that, sometimes, the best growth happens when we're brave enough to start over.

Getting divorced was another turning point. It was one of the hardest decisions I've ever had to make, but I knew staying in a broken relationship wasn't God's plan for me. I had to let go of the picture-perfect American Dream to find the real dream He had for me. Adapting to the single life again wasn't easy—I felt like I was starting from scratch. But in that season of solitude, I learned to love myself again, to dream again, and to trust God's timing in bringing the right people into my life.

Selling the pool home and downsizing into a maintenance-free condo was more than just a real estate transaction—it was a declaration that I was ready to embrace a new season. That home had represented so much: success, stability, and the life I thought I wanted. Letting it go was difficult, but doing so felt like shedding a layer that no longer fit. That downsized condo became a sanctuary, a place where I could rebuild my dreams without the weight of the past.

Choosing community over isolation was another pivotal moment. When life falls apart, it's tempting to withdraw and try to handle everything on your own. But I learned the power of finding my tribe—faith-based groups, church friends, and mentors who believed in me when I struggled to believe in myself. These people became the hands and feet of Jesus, showing me that God doesn't call us to go through hard times alone.

Mentorship and new relationships opened doors I didn't even know were there. I found strength in the wisdom of others, and every time I showed up for a women's event, a networking meeting, or a coffee date with someone who had walked this road before me, I felt God's hand guiding me forward.

Through each pivot—moving to a new city, letting go of relationships, selling a home, finding community—I became a happier, more faith-filled version of myself. Every time I felt lighter after letting something or someone go, it was God's way of letting me know it was the right choice.

These pivotal moments didn't just change my circumstances—they changed me. They reminded me that the only way to truly grow is to let go of what's holding you back, even if it's something you once thought you couldn't live without.

Learning to Love Again

With the freedom I found in my business and a whole lot of heart-healing, I finally felt ready to open my heart to love again. And let me tell you—this season was more challenging than launching multiple businesses.

This time, I wasn't rushing or chasing; I was trusting God to guide me. I prayed for the right partner to walk beside me on this journey. And just like my businesses, relationships came with their own trial and error. I had to lean into God's wisdom to align my choices with His plan for my life.

What I thought I wanted in a partner no longer fit the life I was building. I needed someone who shared my faith, my dreams, and my passion for freedom. As the fairytale goes, you sometimes have to kiss a few frogs before finding your prince.

But in His perfect timing, God led me to the right man—someone I met through an online dating app. Yes, online dating really can work! It's an incredible way to meet people you'd never cross paths with otherwise.

God blessed me with Ryan, a Christian man who shares my entrepreneurial spirit and my love for adventure. We've been happily married for the last three years, and together we're building a life rooted in faith, freedom, and finances that align with our values. We wanted to work around our lives, not live around our work.

After we eloped, we spent three years on the road traveling the USA, visiting over 200 different cities, and creating memories that will last a lifetime. We explored new cities and national parks, and made it a priority to visit friends and family across the country. Living in a tiny house on wheels—our little sanctuary on the road—was both a test and a gift. Being in such a small space challenged us to grow even closer. And let me tell you, if you can live in an RV together without wanting to kill each other, you know you've found your lifelong match!

Today, our life is about choosing to take that leap of faith—to live boldly and embrace the dreams God placed in our hearts. It's about following those dreams, putting in the work to make them a reality, and ensuring that money serves us—so we never miss out on the precious moments that matter most.

As you read this, I hope you feel inspired to ask yourself: What would living differently look like for you? How can you build a life that aligns with your values, passions, and purpose?

Building the Life God Intended for YOU

Now that you've heard my journey, from divorced to dreaming again, I want you to consider this: What story has God planned for you? Every challenge is a chance to make a change and boldly pursue the dreams He has placed in your heart.

Sometimes, all it takes is seeing someone else step out in faith to give you the courage to live the lifestyle you've always wanted. Don't let fear of failure hold you back—be more afraid of never trying.

God has a plan for your life that's bigger than any obstacle you might face. Each pivot, each setback, each leap of faith is part of the story He's writing for you. You are stronger than you think, and you were created for a purpose greater than you could ever imagine.

So let this chapter inspire you to embrace flexibility, let go of what no longer serves you, and step into the life God has been waiting for you to build. The life He intended for you is one filled with purpose, freedom, and blessings beyond measure.

Reflection Questions

- What did "letting go" mean to you in this season?
- How did learning to pivot bring unexpected blessings?
- What obstacles in your life have taught you the most about perseverance?
- When have you had to pivot in a completely new direction?
- How has letting go of control opened new doors in your life?
- Where can you embrace more flexibility and trust God's plan for your future?
- What did each pivot reveal about what you truly value?
- How did these moments set the stage for your reinvention?

CHAPTER 4

Faith as the Foundation — The Cherry on Top of My Sundae

Chapter Overview

This chapter dives deep into the role faith has played in every pivotal moment of my life. It's been the bedrock of my resilience, the unwavering anchor that kept me steady through every storm. Faith is the sweet cherry on top of my PinkPrint journey, adding meaning, purpose, and joy to even the hardest moments. In these pages, I'll share personal stories of Holy Spirit-led decisions, the transformative power of prayer and fasting, financial faithfulness through tithing, and how learning to let go and let God pave the way for every breakthrough.

Letting Go and Letting God

If there's one thing I've learned through all the pivots, detours, and challenges, it's this: faith is the foundation that makes every pivot possible. My journey so far—marked by resilience, perseverance, and learning to embrace change—would have been impossible without the deep, unshakable trust I've placed in God.

I've learned to live by the motto: Let Go and Let God. These words aren't just a saying—they're a lifeline. They've been my guiding light in the darkest nights, the words I've clung to when life seemed to be crumbling around me.

There's only one option when I'm faced with adversity: dust off my shoulders, lean into my faith, and power through it with passion and purpose, knowing God is by my side.

- Let Go and Let God—Surrender the battle to the One who fights for you.
- Struggles Make You Stronger—Every challenge shapes you into the warrior God designed you to be.
- Faith Over Fear—Choose to trust God's plan even when you can't see the outcome.
- Your Setbacks Are Only Setups—Every obstacle is preparing you for the path, purpose, and plan God has for you.

Faith has been the cherry on top of my life's sundae—the sweet final touch that completes the picture. Just like a cherry makes a sundae whole, faith—and the Holy Spirit—add that perfect finishing flourish to every area of my life. And on Sundays, the day I set aside for worship and rest, I'm reminded that God is the cherry on top of every week, too—my source of strength, purpose, and joy.

Trusting Divine Timing

One of the hardest lessons I've learned is to trust God's timing—even when it doesn't align with my own plans. As much as I love setting goals, making lists, and creating schedules, God sometimes steps in and reminds me that His timing is perfect, even when mine feels off-track.

One memorable story that taught me this lesson happened during a trip that didn't go as planned. My flight out of SRQ was delayed due to weather, and I would have missed my connection. Instead of panicking, I leaned into what I've come to call my "faith over fear" mode. I took a deep breath, whispered a quick prayer, and reminded myself that God always has a reason for delays.

As it turned out, United Airlines rebooked me on a different flight—one that left from Tampa instead of Sarasota. I was twelve hours late, leaving from a completely different airport than originally scheduled. But God had a plan for this delay. Along the way, I was blessed by the incredible customer service from a kind agent at United, and I even made a new friend, Chelsea, whom I met at the airport. Chelsea and I shared a taxi ride to Tampa, and over pizza in a hotel restaurant, we shared our stories and dreams. That night reminded me that, sometimes, God uses delays to reroute us—not just physically, but emotionally and spiritually as well.

Waiting on God's timing isn't always easy. Sometimes the hardest part is letting go of your own timeline and trusting that God's plan is always for your good. But when you do, you'll find blessings you could never have orchestrated on your own. Ecclesiastes 3:11 (New International Version) captures it perfectly: "He has made everything beautiful in its time."

Never forget that even the smallest divine delay could be part of God's plan. That red light might have kept you from an accident. That extra meeting time might have introduced you to your next business partner. You could have been put in the right room at the right time to change your entire life. When life gives you lemons, don't let it get you down. Trust in God's plan and make some lemonade out of it. There's always a reason, and you never know how He might use you for His Kingdom. Be grateful and have faith—because His timing is always right on time.

Holy Spirit-Led Decisions

One of the most life-changing lessons I've learned is that the Holy Spirit is my guide, my comforter, and my constant companion through every pivot. Who knows? His voice may be that gentle nudge or that small whisper in your heart, guiding you to take steps that may not always make sense to the world but are perfectly aligned with God's plan.

As a Christian entrepreneur, I've realized that I don't always get to be the boss of my own story. I might have the best business plan, the perfect relationship, or the most detailed to-do list, but God often has the final say—and sometimes, His plan looks nothing like mine.

Think about Mary and Joseph. They had their whole future mapped out—a sweet engagement, a wedding, and a simple, ordinary life together. Then God stepped in and rerouted everything. Mary didn't ask for the Holy Spirit to surprise her with news that would turn her world upside down. Joseph didn't plan on being the stepdad to the Son of God. But they both chose to trust God's plan over their own, even when it didn't make sense.

I've experienced that same kind of Holy Spirit nudge in my own life— times when I felt prompted to take a leap of faith, like leaving a steady corporate job to build a business that aligned with my purpose and calling. It wasn't always easy. But every time I obeyed that prompting, it led to breakthroughs I could never have orchestrated on my own.

Learning to distinguish my own voice from the Holy Spirit's guidance took time and practice. Proverbs 3:5–6 (NIV) reminds us: "Trust in the Lord with all your heart and lean not on your own understanding; in all your ways submit to Him, and He will make your paths straight." These verses became my daily reminder that God's direction is always better than mine—even if it leads me down a path I didn't plan.

Sometimes, God's plan for us is not the easiest path—but it's always the most purposeful. Mary and Joseph's story shows that God's plan can include challenges, delays, and even confusion. But through every obstacle, He's right there with us. Romans 8:28 (NIV) reassures us: "And we know that in all things God works for the good of those who love Him, who have been called according to His purpose." Even when life feels messy or our plans fall apart, God's bigger purpose is still in play.

Every time life threw me a curveball—when a relationship ended, a business deal fell through, or a plan didn't work out—I had a choice: fight it or trust God's redirection. I've learned that when I let go of my own timeline and allow the Holy Spirit to guide me, I end up right where I'm supposed to be. The Holy Spirit in us gives us the power and ability to walk out these steps. Galatians 5:22–23 reminds us that patience is a fruit of the Spirit—something we can develop and grow as we walk by faith.

Faith is believing that God's plan is better than ours, even when it feels like He's messing everything up. But in the end, those divine pivots are the very moments that lead us to the most beautiful breakthroughs—the ones we never saw coming. So when the pivot comes—when the flight is delayed, the business deal changes, or life feels like it's been turned upside down—choose faith over fear. Remember: setbacks are often setups, and the Holy Spirit's guidance is always leading you to something bigger and better than you could have imagined.

Sozo Life Concepts — Healing, Deliverance, Transformation

In my journey of personal and professional growth, I discovered that true transformation begins from within. It's not just about changing circumstances, but about healing the heart, renewing the mind, and aligning with God's purpose. This realization led me to explore the concept of sozo, a Greek word meaning "saved, healed, delivered, preserved, protected, and made whole."

Sozo isn't merely a one-time event; it's an ongoing process of salvation and restoration. As my pastor, Johnny Jones, so powerfully explains in his book *The Sozo Life: How One Question from God Led to My Greatest Discovery*, many believers settle for a "so-so" Christian life, unaware of the full inheritance available through the finished work of Jesus Christ. I highly recommend grabbing a copy of his book if you're ready to dive deeper into what living the sozo life can mean for you.

Engaging with sozo ministry was a pivotal moment in my life. It provided a safe space to confront and release past wounds, negative mindsets, and spiritual strongholds that were holding me back. Through guided sessions, I experienced profound healing and a renewed sense of purpose. This inner transformation empowered me to embrace life's pivots with confidence and clarity.

Living a sozo life means daily walking in the fullness of salvation. It's about healing, deliverance, and transformation. Romans 12:2 (NIV) reminds us: "Do not conform to the pattern of this world, but be transformed by the renewing of your mind." This transformation is what allows us to embrace the pivots God places before us, trusting that He is making all things new.

Prayer, Fasting, and Giving

When life felt uncertain or overwhelming, prayer, fasting, and giving became my go-to tools for clarity, strength, and breakthrough. They weren't just spiritual disciplines—they were lifelines that anchored my faith and opened doors for God's blessings in ways I never expected.

Prayer taught me to bring every need—big or small—before God. It became my safe space to pour out my heart, share my worries, and seek His wisdom. Whether I was deciding on a business opportunity, working through relationship challenges, or simply asking for strength, prayer kept me connected to God's guidance. Prayer is a conversation that invites God into every detail of our lives, reminding us that He cares about every aspect of our journey. Philippians 4:6–7 (NIV) says, "Do not be anxious about anything, but in every situation, by prayer and petition, with thanksgiving, present your requests to God. And the peace of God, which transcends all understanding, will guard your hearts and your minds in Christ Jesus." These verses remind me that prayer is not just about asking—it's about trusting.

Fasting became a powerful tool whenever I needed to break through spiritual or practical roadblocks. I discovered that fasting isn't just about giving up food; it's about clearing the clutter and making room for God to move. I've done several 24 to 48-hour water fasts during times when I needed clarity on big decisions or a breakthrough in areas where I felt stuck. One of the most transformative fasts I did wasn't about food at all—it was a 9-month fast from TV. That simple sacrifice gave me time to walk three miles every day, improve my health, and build three new income streams. It didn't just change my schedule—it changed my life.

Giving—whether it's time, talent, or treasure—has a way of shifting our perspective from scarcity to abundance. At the heart of giving is tithing, the practice of giving God the first 10% of our income. Tithing wasn't just a financial checkbox for me; it was an act of trust and obedience that put God first in every part of my life. Malachi 3:10 (NIV) says, "Bring the whole tithe into the storehouse, that there may be food in my house. Test Me in this and see if I will not throw open the floodgates of heaven and pour out so much blessing that there will not be room enough to store it." Even when giving felt like a stretch, God always proved faithful.

Tithing taught me to see Him—not my paycheck—as my true provider. It reminded me that He alone gives us the power to create wealth, and that our financial blessings are meant to honor Him and advance His kingdom. Proverbs 3:9–10 (New Living Translation) says, "Honor the Lord with your wealth and with the best part of everything you produce. Then He will fill your barns with grain, and your vats will overflow with good wine." Giving God our best—our first fruits—invites Him into every part of our finances and opens the door for blessings we couldn't imagine.

Through prayer, fasting, and giving, I've experienced firsthand how God can take what we sacrifice and multiply it beyond anything we could ever ask or imagine. These practices didn't just help me survive tough seasons—they helped me thrive and grow stronger in faith, resilience, and purpose.

Weaving Faith Through Every Pivot

Faith wasn't just a footnote in my journey—it was the fuel behind every decision, every pivot, every comeback. It's what turned obstacles into opportunities and setbacks into setups. When things didn't make sense, faith reminded me that God always has a bigger plan. When the path ahead felt uncertain, faith became my anchor and my compass.

Every pivot I made—whether it was letting go of toxic relationships, embracing new business ventures, or stepping into the unknown—was strengthened by the trust that God was guiding me. I've learned that when God is at the center, no challenge is wasted. Every struggle, every triumph, every detour has a divine purpose.

My hope for you is that you'll see your faith as the key to unlocking your own PinkPrint—the blueprint for turning life's lemons into the sweetest pink lemonade. Let your faith be the thread that weaves resilience, joy, and abundance into every chapter of your story.

Just like a cherry on top of a sundae, faith is that final flourish that completes the sweet life God has promised. It's the finishing touch that brings it all together. It's also a reminder that on Sundays—the day I set aside for worship, reflection, and rest—I give God the first and best part of my week, trusting Him to bless and complete the rest.

When you place God at the center of every pivot, you'll find that even the hardest seasons can produce the most beautiful harvests. Keep trusting, keep praying, and keep moving forward. Your journey is unfolding just as it should—one faith-filled step at a time.

Reflection Questions

- How has your faith been tested in times of change?
- When have you felt the Holy Spirit guiding your decisions?
- Where might God be asking you to trust Him more deeply right now?

CHAPTER 5

The Power PinkPrint — From Unstoppable Woman to Unshakable Success

Chapter Overview

This chapter introduces you to the PinkPrint, my signature five-step system that blends faith, mindset, strategy, and community. It's the step-by-step guide I developed from my own journey—designed to help you transform your challenges into opportunities and build the life you're called to live. We'll unpack each step, integrate the SUCCESS acronym, and share practical strategies to empower you to thrive, no matter what life throws your way.

Introduction: From Unstoppable Woman to Unshakable Success

By now, you've seen the power of resilience, the strength of faith, and the art of pivoting in action. You've walked with me through the ups and downs of my journey—from the challenges that forced me to grow, to the moments that revealed who I really am. Every setback, every pivot, and every breakthrough was building something bigger than I could have imagined.

That "something bigger" is what I call the PinkPrint—a roadmap for turning life's toughest lemons into the sweetest pink lemonade. It's more than a catchy name. It's the system that took me from feeling lost and broken to becoming the unshakable, faith-filled woman I am today. This PinkPrint didn't just transform my life—it rebuilt my business, strengthened my faith, and gave me the courage to live out my God-given purpose.

I created the PinkPrint based on real-life experience, not theory. It's the blueprint I used to navigate divorce, career pivots, and financial reinvention. It's the step-by-step process I leaned on every time I faced an obstacle that could have taken me down.

And now, it's yours.

This chapter is your invitation to build your own PinkPrint—a personalized guide that empowers you to face any challenge, pivot with purpose, and create the success story God wrote just for you. It's time to step into your power, embrace your faith, and become the unstoppable woman you were born to be.

Are you ready to build a life you love, filled with faith, resilience, and unshakable success? Let's get started.

Mindset Reset

Every transformation begins in the mind. Before you can build the life of your dreams, you have to clear out the clutter—doubt, fear, and limiting beliefs that hold you back. This is where the PinkPrint journey begins: with a mindset reset.

Let's be honest—life will always throw us lemons. From heartbreak to career pivots, self-doubt is often the loudest voice in the room. I've faced those moments—the late nights questioning my decisions, the times when it felt like everyone else had it figured out but me. But I learned that every breakthrough starts by rewiring how you think.

A mindset reset means being intentional about what you allow to take root in your mind. It's about transforming "I can't." into "God's got this." When my world felt like it was crumbling, these three tools became my lifeline—the anchors that kept me moving forward even when the path was uncertain.

Mel Robbins 5-4-3-2-1 Rule

Fear has a funny way of paralyzing us right when we're about to step into something big. That's why I love Mel Robbins' 5-4-3-2-1 Rule. It's like a rocket launch for your dreams. When fear, doubt, or hesitation shows up, count backward—5-4-3-2-1—and **GO**.

This simple countdown helps snap you out of analysis paralysis and puts you into motion. I've used it to send that email I was scared to write, make the phone call I was avoiding, and hit "publish" on posts that made me vulnerable. Each time felt like a victory over the fear that wanted to hold me back.

Don't let your mind talk you out of your goals. Don't overthink. Just move.

Ready, Set, Go (Oola)

Introduced to me by the Oola team, this three-step process turns obstacles into opportunities:

- **Ready:** Acknowledge the obstacle exists. Name it—fear of failure, imposter syndrome, or a toxic relationship.
- **Set:** Ask yourself, "What happens if I overcome this? What if I give up?" Detailing both outcomes refocuses your mind on possibility rather than paralysis.
- **Go:** Claim twenty seconds of courage and take action. That single step breaks the cycle of doubt and propels you toward your goal.

I've used Ready, Set, Go in launching businesses, rebuilding finances, and healing relationships. It's a personal roadmap for the messy middle—when you're between where you are and where God is calling you to be.

Steve Harvey's Jump Theory

I'll never forget the first time I heard Steve Harvey talk about his Jump Theory. He said, "You have to jump. If you don't jump, you'll never soar." That hit me hard because I knew I'd spent too much time standing on the edge, waiting for the perfect conditions.

Steve's wisdom is simple: you have to be willing to leap before you feel ready. The parachute might not open right away—you might bump onto a few cliffs on the way down—but eventually, it will. And in that free fall, you'll learn to trust and put your faith in God more than ever.

I've jumped into new careers, new relationships, new adventures, even when the landing felt uncertain. And every time, God caught me. Not always the way I expected, but always at the right time.

How I Put It All Together

These three methods—5-4-3-2-1, Ready Set Go, and Jump—aren't just theories. They're the tools I use to reset my mindset, trade doubt for determination, and keep moving when fear tries to stop me. Every pivot, every breakthrough, every step in my PinkPrint started with a mindset reset. Because if you can win the battle in your mind, you can conquer anything the world throws your way.

So ask yourself:

- What obstacles are standing in my way?
- Am I ready to count backward, ask the hard questions, and jump?
- Am I willing to trust that God's timing is always better than my own?

Your dreams are waiting on the other side of a mindset reset. And with these tools, you're more than equipped to cross that bridge. Let's go!

Attribution & Fair Use Notice

In crafting the PinkPrint system, I've drawn on—and adapted—several proven methods. To respect the original creators and maintain legal clarity:

- **Mel Robbins 5-4-3-2-1 Rule**: Summarized and attributed to Mel Robbins. No extensive quotes are reproduced.
- **Oola's Ready, Set, Go Framework**: Credited to the founders of Oola, described in my own words without reproducing proprietary materials or trademarks beyond the name.
- **Steve Harvey's Jump Theory**: Paraphrased from Steve Harvey's public teachings.

These adaptations qualify as fair use. They are brief, properly credited, and integrated into a unique, transformative framework centered on faith and personal narrative. No endorsement by Mel Robbins, Oola, or Steve Harvey is implied; all trademarks remain the property of their respective owners.

Faith Over Fear

When I look back at every major pivot in my life, one thing stands out: faith was always my anchor, holding me steady when fear threatened to pull me under. Whether I was standing at the edge of divorce, staring at a "You're laid off" letter, or contemplating a brand-new business venture, faith whispered, "You can do this," even when my heart screamed, "What if I fail?"

Choosing Faith in the Darkest Moments

After my divorce, I woke up each morning with a knot of anxiety in my chest. But instead of letting fear dictate my next move, I decided to lean unto faith. I'd start my day reading a Psalm—reminding myself that God walks beside me even in the valley. One verse became my battle cry: "Even though I walk through the darkest valley, I will fear no evil, for you are with me." (Ps. 23:4 NIV). With that promise tucked in my heart, I found the courage to list my dream house for sale, downsize my life, and trust God's plan for a fresh start.

When my corporate role ended, it would have been easy to panic. Instead, I claimed God's promise to provide (Matt. 6:31–33) and launched my first side business. I spent quiet mornings praying over my computer screen, asking God to guide my strategy. Within weeks, my new venture began generating income—proof that faith truly does move mountains.

Faith-Fueled Growth in Business and Relationships

Building multiple income streams—everything from e-commerce to coaching—required risk. Each time I hesitated, I reminded myself that God calls us to walk by faith, not by sight (2 Cor. 5:7). When I hesitated to invest in paid advertising, I prayed for confidence, set a small budget, and watched God turn that seed into a harvest.

Relationships, too, were transformed by faith. After I remarried, my husband and I spent months in small RV quarters—an invitation for fear to whisper, "This will never work." Instead, we chose faith. I prayed every morning, leaned on our church family for support, and watched God turn cramped space into deeper intimacy.

Practical Tips to Cultivate Faith Over Fear

1. **Daily Prayer Practice**
    Begin each day with a two-minute prayer: thank God for yesterday's victories, present today's worries, and ask for courage.

2. **Scripture Study**
    Pick a verse that addresses your current fear (e.g., Isaiah 41:10, Philippians 4:13) and journal how it speaks into your situation.

3. **Faith-Based Community**
    Join a small group or Bible study. Share your fears openly and receive encouragement. Accountability from sisters in faith turns doubt into determination.

4. **Remember Past Faithfulness**
    Keep a "faith journal" of answered prayers. On hard days, revisit those entries to remind yourself that God has never failed you.

5. **Speak Truth Over Fear**

    When fear arises, counter it immediately with a declaration: "God is my provider," "I can do all things through Christ," or another promise that fits your struggle.

Faith isn't wishful thinking—it's the fuel that empowers each step you take. When you choose faith over fear, you ignite a force that carries you through every storm. As you continue your PinkPrint journey, let faith light the way, knowing that God has already gone before you, preparing a path to unshakable success.

Dream Big, Goal Small

Are you tired of declaring, "This is my year!" only to watch your resolutions fizzle out by February? Do you feel overwhelmed by the gap between where you are and where you want to be? You're not alone—and you're in the right place. Every woman holds within her the seeds of greatness, but those seeds need a nurturing plan to grow. That's why the PinkPrint calls you to **dream big** and **goal small**.

Crafting Your Vision Board

Since 2018, I've attended an annual dream-building conference where women spend two days soul-searching, dreaming, and yes—sometimes even crying—over exactly where we are, where we want to go, and how we'll get there. One of the most powerful tools we use is the **vision board**.

A vision board is more than a collage of images; it's a dynamic canvas for your hopes and dreams. Each picture, quote, or symbol you choose should spark excitement and align with your deepest desires. Unstoppable women carve out dedicated time—away from distractions—to curate and arrange these elements. When you hang your vision board in a prominent spot, it serves as a daily reminder of what you're aiming for, keeping your aspirations at the forefront of your mind.

Setting Clear and Specific S.M.A.R.T. Goals

Big dreams need bite-sized milestones. That's where the **S.M.A.R.T. method** comes in:

- **Specific:** Pinpoint exactly what you want.
- **Measurable:** Attach numbers or dates so you know when you've succeeded.
- **Accountable:** Share your goals with someone who can check in on your progress.
- **Realistic:** Aim high, but stay grounded in what you can achieve with effort.
- **Time-bound:** Set a clear deadline to keep yourself motivated.

For example, instead of "I want to get healthy," try "I will walk three miles every Monday, Wednesday, and Friday morning for the next three months." This level of clarity transforms fluffy wishes into concrete targets you can pursue with confidence.

Taking Consistent, Purposeful Action

Goals without action are just daydreams. The most successful women I know break big objectives into daily habits:

1. **Daily To-Do's:** List two to three tasks each morning that align with your bigger vision.
2. **Time Blocking:** Dedicate specific windows for focus—whether it's brainstorming your next blog post or practicing a new skill.
3. **Discipline Over Motivation:** Motivation ebbs and flows; discipline carries you forward when you don't "feel like it."

Remember, progress isn't always a straight line. You'll face setbacks. When that happens, pivot, learn, and keep moving. The unstoppable woman treats challenges as feedback, not failure.

Celebrating Milestones

Every small win fuels your momentum. Did you complete your first week of evening walks? Treat yourself to something that reminds you of your why—a healthy smoothie, a new journal, a quiet moment of gratitude. Celebrations reinforce positive habits and remind you that you're on the right track.

One Step at a Time

Your PinkPrint is a living roadmap. You'll dream big—envisioning that life-changing new career, book deal, or ministry opportunity—while setting achievable steps that lead you there. Keep your eyes on the horizon, but take it one footstep at a time.

Reflection Questions

- What does your dream life look like in vivid detail?
- How can you apply the S.M.A.R.T. framework to your biggest goal?
- What small action can you take tomorrow that moves you closer to your vision?

You have everything you need to transform your dreams into reality. Dream boldly, plan wisely, and take that first small step today. Your unstoppable future awaits.

Network Power

No woman succeeds alone. Throughout my journey, I discovered that the relationships we cultivate are just as vital as the strategies we employ. Community, mentorship, and authentic connections became the wind beneath my wings—lifting me higher than I ever could have flown on my own.

After my divorce, I stepped into singleness feeling like I was starting over. Then I found a faith-based young adults group that became my spiritual family. Weekly gatherings turned into deep friendships that held me accountable to my goals and prayed me through every setback. They celebrated my victories, challenged my thinking, and simply showed up when I needed encouragement the most.

When I ventured into entrepreneurship, I joined both in-person and online networking groups. Seasoned business owners generously shared insights I could never have learned from a textbook. Their mentorship gave me the courage to launch new ventures with confidence instead of fear, knowing I had a community cheering me on.

My dream-building journey also led me to the annual Oolapalooza conference. Two full days of workshops, vision-casting, and raw vulnerability transformed my mindset. Standing among hundreds of like-minded women, I realized my story mattered—and that by sharing my struggles, I could inspire others to keep going.

Embrace Accountability and Support

Surrounding yourself with a supportive community can exponentially accelerate your progress. Here's how to tap into that power:

- **Find an Accountability Partner:** Choose someone who shares your values and aspirations. Schedule weekly check-ins to review goals, celebrate wins, and troubleshoot challenges.
- **Join Faith-Based Groups:** Whether at your church or online, a faith community prays for you through tough seasons and rejoices with you in triumphs.

- **Attend Workshops & Networking Events:** Invest in learning and connection. Every conversation can spark your next big idea or business partnership.
- **Give Back:** Community is reciprocal. Offer your expertise, encouragement, or prayer to others; the support you give will come back to you in unexpected ways.

Creating a Ripple Effect

Unstoppable success isn't just about personal achievement; it's about empowering others. As you break barriers and transcend limiting beliefs, your journey becomes a roadmap for women walking a similar path.

- **Share Your Story:** Vulnerability breeds connection. When you speak openly about your highs and lows, you invite others to do the same.
- **Mentor with Intentionality:** As you grow, extend a hand to someone who is just starting out. Your guidance could be the catalyst for her own breakthrough.
- **Invest in Your Community:** Lead a workshop, host a small group, or simply pray for a friend. Your impact ripples far beyond your immediate circle.

Your network is more than a list of contacts—it's the fertile soil where dreams take root and flourish. Surround yourself with champions, lean on mentors, and offer your own support. Together, you'll create a legacy of empowerment that transforms not just your life, but the lives of countless others.

Action Over Analysis

One of the biggest dream killers is overthinking. We can research, refine, and re-refine until the excitement fades, but then, the perfect moment never comes. Faith without works is dead (Jas. 2:17). Action is the bridge between vision and reality.

As a recovering perfectionist, I know this struggle all too well. I spent weeks taking courses, listening to seminars, and tweaking every detail—convinced that my launch had to be flawless. It wasn't until I prayed for clarity that I realized perfection would never get the job done. So when my sister, Heather, finally called me out: "Tara, it doesn't have to be perfect, it just has to be done," I built a simple landing page, hit "publish," and sent a straightforward email invite to my network. The freedom I felt from breaking analysis paralysis was life-changing. That moment taught me that **"doing the thing,"** even imperfectly, creates unstoppable momentum.

Overthinking breeds paralysis. You tell yourself you need more data, more research, or more resources—meanwhile, opportunities slip away. Instead, combine faith and action. Commit your work to the Lord, and your plans will be established (Prov. 16:3). When you act in faith, you trust God to guide your next steps as you move forward.

Practical Tips to Embrace Action Over Analysis

- **Create a Simple Plan:** Identify your core objective and list three small steps you can take this week.
- **Take the First Imperfect Step:** Launch a draft landing page, send a quick email, or record a short video—no more waiting for "perfect."
- **Set a Deadline:** Use a countdown (5-4-3-2-1 or Ready, Set, Go) to switch from planning to doing.
- **Seek Rapid Feedback:** Share your initial version with a trusted mentor or accountability partner, then refine based on real input.
- **Adjust as needed:** Use real-world feedback to improve your work rather than waiting for flawless conditions.

Every moment spent planning without action is a moment lost. Step out in faith, take that imperfect first step, and watch how action unlocks opportunities you never imagined.

The SUCCESS Acronym

As a bonus framework to reinforce your PinkPrint steps, I use the **SUCCESS** acronym. Each letter reminds you of a key mindset or action that turns ordinary goals into extraordinary breakthroughs.

S — Set Your Goals

Create a vivid mental picture of what you want to achieve and write it down. I still remember sketching out my "dream life" after Oolapalooza—writing out exactly what I wanted to do and the bite-sized steps on how I would get there. That exercise gave clarity I carried into every decision.

U — Understand the Obstacles

Identify barriers that might stand in your way and plan how to overcome them. When I first launched my Airbnb business, I listed every fear—finances, regulations, competition—and then tackled them one by one (research zoning laws, set a strict budget, study market trends).

C — Create a Positive Mental Picture

Visualize yourself succeeding; align your thoughts with your faith. Before every big launch, I spend sixty seconds picturing a packed calendar of happy clients and praising God for provision long before it arrives.

C — Clear Your Mind of Self-Doubt

Let go of the fears and lies that hold you back. I used to believe "I'm not enough" until I wrote that lie on a sticky note, ripped it up, and taped a Bible verse—"I can do all things through Christ who strengthens me." (Phil. 4:13 New King James Version)—in its place.

E — Embrace the Challenge

See obstacles as opportunities to grow stronger. When my first course sold fewer spots than I hoped, I rewrote the curriculum instead of quitting—and it doubled registrations the next month.

S — Stay on Track

Stay committed, even when it's hard. I block every Monday morning in my calendar for "Vision Review"—a 15-minute check-in to celebrate wins, adjust goals, and pray for the week ahead.

S — Show the World You Can Do It

Let your light shine and be an example to others. After nailing my first live webinar—despite technical glitches—I shared the recording along with a candid post about what went wrong. That authenticity drew more bookings than any perfect promo ever could.

Reflection Questions

- Which SUCCESS step feels most natural—and which requires the most courage?
- How can you weave at least two of these letters into your daily routine this week?
- What's one small action you'll take today to move from "seeing" your goals to making them a reality?

Putting Your PinkPrint into Practice

You now have the tools, the framework, and the faith to turn your biggest dreams into reality. To help you move from inspiration to implementation, here are six practical strategies to integrate into your daily life:

- **Life Audit**
  Regularly assess how you spend your time, where your energy goes, and which habits serve your vision. Trim what drains you, and invest more in activities that fuel your purpose.

- **Mindset Shifts**
  When challenges arise, reframe them as opportunities to grow. Every setback holds a lesson—ask, "How is this making me stronger or wiser?"

- **Environment Design**
  Create a workspace and home life that supports positivity and productivity. Declutter your desk, add inspiring visuals, or set aside a quiet corner just for prayer and planning.

- **Mentorship**
  Seek out mentors and a faith-filled community. Their wisdom, encouragement, and accountability will accelerate your progress and keep you grounded in your values.

- **Storytelling**
  Share your journey openly. Your testimony of perseverance, pivots, and faith not only cements your own resilience but also inspires others to pursue their own PinkPrint.

- **Trust the Process**
  Success rarely arrives overnight. Lean into faith, exercise patience, and persevere through every season. Remember that each small step, taken consistently, leads to unshakable results.

Reflection Questions

- How does your current mindset align with the life you want to create?
- Where have you let fear hold you back, and how can faith lead you forward?
- What big dream do you want to break into small, actionable goals?

- Who can you lean on for support and accountability as you build your PinkPrint?
- What's one step you can take today to move from analysis to action?
- How can the SUCCESS acronym guide your journey to unstoppable success?

Your PinkPrint is more than a plan—it's a living roadmap powered by faith, action, and community. Keep these strategies close, revisit your reflections often, and watch as God transforms your boldest dreams into glorious reality.

CHAPTER 6

Building Your Lemonade Stand— Turning Ideas into Income

Introduction: The Lemonade Stand Metaphor

Think back to the joy of setting up a lemonade stand as a child—mixing tart lemons with sweet sugar, arranging your jars just so, and greeting every passerby with a smile. Running a business isn't so different. A successful venture begins with a clear recipe, careful preparation, and the courage to share your product with the world.

Your "stand" is more than a physical location or website. It is the unique space where you showcase your value, your gifts, and your passion. It is where your customers—whether clients, readers, or students—come to taste the difference only you can offer.

In this chapter, you will learn how to:

1. Find your perfect recipe by identifying the skills and passions that set you apart.
2. Set up your stand with solid business foundations, from legal structure to branding.
3. Serve multiple flavors by building diverse income streams that work together.
4. Scale your operation by automating systems, delegating tasks, and expanding into new markets.

Just like a child with a simple stand on a summer day, you have everything you need to start small and grow big. Let's mix up your first batch of pink lemonade and watch God multiply every cup.

Finding Your Perfect Recipe—Defining Your Unique Value

Every standout lemonade blend starts with a recipe that no one else can replicate. In the world of business, your recipe is your **Unique Value Proposition (UVP)**—the combination of skills, passions, and perspective that only you bring to the table.

What makes your pink lemonade special?

- Is it a flavor no one else offers? Maybe, you blend uncommon fruit or add an unexpected herbal twist.
- In business terms, perhaps it's your deep expertise in financial empowerment, your gift for storytelling, or your faith-driven coaching style.

Exercise: List Your Top Ingredients

Grab a notebook and write down the following:

1. **Three Skills:** What are you exceptionally good at? (e.g., communication, financial analysis, creative design)
2. **Three Passions:** What activities light you up? (e.g., teaching, travel, mentoring)
3. **Three Market Needs:** What problems do you see around you that need solving? (e.g., time management for busy moms, spiritual encouragement for entrepreneurs, simple investing guidance)

Look for overlaps—the intersections where your skills meet your passions and serve a real need. That sweet spot is your signature recipe.

Monetize What You're Already Doing

One mentor once told me, "Your passion often hides in what you already do for free." Think about the tasks you love so much that you volunteer for them, whether it's mentoring a friend, organizing community events, or sharing financial tips with your network. Those free acts are clues to your UVP—turn them into a business offering by packaging your existing gifts into products or services people will pay for.

Aligning Your Gifts with God's Calling

Your unique blend isn't an accident—it's God's design. When you align your UVP with His calling, you'll find both purpose and profit in your stand:

- **Pray for Clarity:** Ask God to confirm which ingredients He's gifted you.
- **Seek Confirmation:** Talk with mentors, friends, or your church community—ask how they've seen you shine.

- **Trust the Process:** Your recipe may evolve. Stay flexible, listen to feedback, and let God refine your blend over time.

By defining and owning your Unique Value Proposition—especially by monetizing what you already do for free—you set your lemonade stand apart, ready to serve customers with flavor only you can deliver.

Choosing Your Ingredients—Skillsets, Passions, and Market Demand

Before you mix up your first batch of pink lemonade, you need to gather the right ingredients—your unique skillsets, passions, and a clear understanding of what the market needs. This ensures your offering isn't just delicious, but also in high demand.

Conduct a Self-Audit

1. **List Your Talents:** Write down everything you do well—public speaking, financial planning, design, coaching.
2. **Document Your Credentials:** Note any licenses or certifications you hold. (e.g., life insurance, real estate, coaching credentials)
3. **Capture Your Interests:** Identify activities that energize you—mentoring, writing, teaching, organizing.

Research Market Gaps & Customer Pain Points

1. **Survey Your Community:** Poll friends, family, or social-media followers. Ask, "What's your biggest challenge around [your expertise]?"
2. **Explore Online Forums:** Browse Facebook groups, Reddit threads, and industry forums to spot recurring questions or complaints.

3. **Study Competitors:** Read reviews on Amazon, Yelp, or industry blogs to uncover unmet needs.

Every piece of feedback is a lemon waiting to be squeezed into a sweeter solution.

Match Ingredients to High-Demand Niches

- **Find the Overlap:** Draw three circles—Skills, Passions, and Market Needs. Where they intersect is your sweet spot.
  - **Example:** I realized my expertise in mindset resets, my skill at building multiple income streams, and my passion for teaching all came together in my "Money Mindset Membership," a program that guides women to diversify and grow their revenue sources.
- **Validate Before You Scale:** Test your idea with a small offering—like a mini-workshop or introductory webinar—and see how your audience responds.

When your gifts, your passions, and a real-world need align, you've found an unbeatable recipe. Your lemonade stand is ready to open—one irresistible flavor at a time.

Setting Up Your Stand—Business Foundations

Before you pour your first cup of pink lemonade, you need a solid foundation beneath your feet. These core elements ensure your business is protected, compliant, and ready to grow.

Legal Structure: Sole Proprietor vs. LLC

- **Sole Proprietor:** Easiest to set up—ideal for testing your idea. You report business income on your personal tax return, but your personal assets carry the liability.

- **LLC (Limited Liability Company):** Adds protection by separating your personal and business assets. You'll file separate paperwork and pay state fees, but you'll sleep better knowing your home and savings are shielded.

Tip: Consult a trusted accountant or attorney to decide which structure fits your goals and risk tolerance.

Finances & Credit: Startup Capital and Separation

- **Good Credit for Startup Capital:** Leverage personal or business credit lines to fund initial expenses—equipment, marketing, and inventory.
- **Separate Accounts:** Open a dedicated business bank account and credit card to keep personal and business cash flow distinct. This simplifies bookkeeping and strengthens your professional image.

Basic Compliance: Licenses, Insurance, and Taxes

- **Licenses & Permits:** Depending on your state and your offerings, you may need a general business license, professional certification, or health permits (for food-related ventures).
- **Insurance:** Protect your stand with general liability insurance; consider professional liability if you offer consulting or coaching.
- **Tax Considerations:** Register for an EIN (Employer Identification Number), collect sales tax if required, and set aside a percentage of revenue for quarterly taxes.

"Stand Design": Branding Basics

- **Name & Logo:** Choose a memorable, authentic name that reflects your UVP. Invest in a simple logo that works across social media, packaging, and signage.

- **Values Statement:** Declare your mission—why you're in business and how you serve your customers. This statement will guide every decision, from marketing copy to product development.

Workbook Resource

I've created a detailed workbook on proper business structuring and building business credit. You can purchase and download it anytime at **bornagainbossbabe.com** to walk through each step in depth.

Serving Multiple Flavors—Building Diverse Revenue Streams

I learned the hard way that relying on a single paycheck is risky. When I was laid off from my Corporate America job without notice, I vowed to never again to put all my eggs in one basket. That moment sparked my journey to build multiple streams of income—one "flavor" at a time—each aligned with the unique values and talents God has given me.

Because one of my core values is **time and location flexibility**, I focused on online and financial income streams that allow me to work anywhere with an internet connection. It's crucial to build your flavors around the lifestyle you want to achieve—something we'll explore in more detail later in this chapter.

If any of these flavors pique your interest, I'm actively looking for **affiliates** who want to plug into my prebuilt businesses and kick off their own Bo$$Babe journey. I'm here to guide and mentor you as you discover the income streams that best suit your strengths and calling. Visit **bornagainbossbabe.com** or reach out on Facebook to learn more and get started, and for anything additional I may have added since this publication.

Forex & Crypto Trading Automation

When I first discovered **automated trading**, it felt like stepping into a whole new world of possibilities. After getting laid off, I knew I never wanted to rely on a single paycheck again—but I also didn't want to hustle 24/7 and miss out on the life I was rebuilding. I wanted *smart* income, not just *hard* income. That's when I found out you could actually let your money work *for* you—even while you sleep.

Forex and crypto trading automation uses software (called bots or EAs) that enters trades on your behalf based on pre-set market strategies. It's not "get rich quick"—but it *is* one of the most powerful ways to tap into the financial markets without needing to stare at charts all day.

I remember the first time I saw a small profit hit my account—and I hadn't touched a thing. It wasn't about the dollar amount. It was about what it *represented*: freedom, confidence, and a quiet moment of peace knowing I had options again.

What It Is:

Automated systems that buy and sell forex, gold, or crypto based on market signals. Once it's set up, it can run 24/5—even when you're traveling, working your 9 to 5, or spending time with your family.

Why It Matters:

- **Time freedom:** No more trading hours glued to the screen.
- **Stress relief:** You don't have to be an expert—let the data do the work.
- **Passive power:** It's like setting up a digital worker who never sleeps, doesn't call in sick, and never needs a vacation.

Getting Started:

1. **Open a trading account** with a reputable broker that supports automation.
2. **Choose a trading strategy or bot**—I'll even introduce you to the ones I use.
3. **Test first** with demo funds (always!). Then go live when you're ready.

Time vs. Money:

You'll spend time upfront researching bots or mentors—but once it's running, it requires very little daily attention. It's perfect for busy moms, side-hustlers, or anyone who wants to earn *without* adding more to their plate.

Keys to Profitability:

- Use risk settings that protect your account, not gamble with it.
- Check in weekly—don't set it and forget it completely.
- Partner with someone who's already walked this path so you don't have to learn the hard way (ask me how!).

Real Talk:

This isn't just about profit margins. It's about peace of mind. It's about knowing that when life throws you another curveball, you've got something *already moving* in your favor. Trading bots gave me more than passive income—they gave me margin for the moments that matter.

Forex & Crypto Education and Trading: Learn the Skill, Keep the Freedom

There's a level of confidence that comes from knowing you can make money anywhere in the world—on your own time, using your own skillset. **Trading gave me that confidence**, and now I want to pass that same power on to you.

At first, I was intimidated by trading. It felt like a foreign language filled with charts, candlesticks, and confusing strategies. But once I found the right mentors, tools, and beginner-friendly education, it all started to click.

And here's what I want you to know, sis:
Trading doesn't have to be scary.

You don't need to be good at math. You don't need a finance degree. You don't even have to spend hours glued to a screen. You just need a desire to learn and a willingness to show up.

With the **right resources and step-by-step guidance**, you can take control of your financial future and start earning even while you're still learning.

What It Is:

Learning how to trade in the foreign exchange (forex) and cryptocurrency markets by accessing beginner-friendly resources—like live sessions, strategy breakdowns, and simple explanations—so you can start building skill and confidence, one trade at a time.

Why It Matters:

- **It's flexible.** You can trade from your phone or laptop, day or night—whenever it fits your life.
- **It's portable.** Whether you're at home, traveling, or in between jobs, all you need is Wi-Fi.
- **It's empowering.** Learning how to multiply your money is a skill that no one can take from you.

This is about **freedom**, not perfection. It's about equipping yourself with a high-income skill that aligns with your values, your goals, and your vision for the future.

Getting Started:

1. **Plug into my beginner-friendly trading resources** that are designed to simplify the process and support you at every step.
2. **Practice in a demo account** to gain confidence before going live.
3. **Join a community** where you're not alone—ask questions, celebrate wins, and learn side by side with others.
4. **Set your own pace.** This is your journey, and you get to decide how fast or slow you go.

Time vs. Money:

Trading does take time to learn, but you can do it in small pockets of your day. It doesn't require a huge investment upfront—and once you find your rhythm, it becomes one of the most **flexible and scalable** income streams available.

Keys to Success:

- **Stay consistent.** It's not about big wins overnight—it's about building skill daily.
- **Start small.** Even ten dollar trades can teach you priceless lessons.
- **Use the right tools.** Avoid YouTube rabbit holes. Stick with trusted resources that are beginner-proof and results-focused.
- **Don't do it alone.** Surround yourself with others on the same journey—it makes all the difference.

Real Talk:

A new level of confidence. A new stream of income. A new sense of control.

I never thought my own trading story would become someone else's breakthrough. But when you show up to educate with integrity and passion, people *feel it.* They follow you not just because of the money, but because of the mission.

I've had women tell me, *"Tara, I've been praying for someone to teach me this."* That's when I knew this wasn't just business. This was ministry too.

If you're ready to explore trading but don't know where to start, I've got you. I'll share the same tools, strategies, and simple steps I used to go from confused to confident in the market.

You can message me on Facebook or visit bornagainbossbabe.com to get plugged into the exact resources I use.

E-Commerce Stores (Amazon, eBay, Facebook Marketplace):

Turning Products into Purpose and Packages into Paychecks
When I first started selling online, I didn't know if anyone would buy from me. I wasn't a tech wizard. I didn't have fancy systems. But what I *did* have was hustle, faith, and a desire to create more margin—margin in my time, my finances, and my life.

E-commerce became my quiet blessing. It gave me the ability to earn while I slept, while I traveled, and even while I prayed. Every product I shipped, every sale that came in, reminded me that I didn't need to punch a clock to prosper. I just needed to *start*—and be willing to learn the systems.

If you're someone who's already recommending your favorite products to friends, then, why not get paid for it? If you're already scrolling through Facebook Marketplace, then, why not list an item instead of just liking one?

This is for the woman who wants a tangible, flexible income stream—one she can run from her phone, from the passenger seat of her RV, or from her kitchen counter while the kids nap.

What It Is:

Selling physical products on trusted marketplaces like Amazon, eBay, and Facebook Marketplace. You don't need a huge warehouse or a private label brand to begin. You can start by reselling items you already own or sourcing budget-friendly treasures that people are *already searching for*.

Why It Matters:

- It puts control back in your hands. You choose the products, the prices, and the pace.
- It's flexible. Whether you have five hours a week or two hours a day, there's a model that fits your schedule.
- It gives you proof that profits don't require a 9 to 5—just resourcefulness and a little strategy.
- It lets you turn clutter into cash—literally. That shelf of unused gadgets? Someone's searching for them right now.

Getting Started:

1. **Pick Your Platform:** Start with choosing a platform (like Facebook Marketplace for instant local flips or Amazon for national reach).

2. **Source Products:** Find products you can sell from clearance aisles, thrift stores, garage sales, or even your own home (this is called retail arbitrage).
3. **Create Your Listings:** Take great photos, write clear descriptions, and use searchable keywords to boost your products' visibility.
4. **Fulfill Orders:** Ship items promptly, respond to customer inquiries, and ask for reviews to build credibility.

Time vs. Money:

E-commerce does require some time upfront—especially when learning how to source, photograph, and list items well. But the beauty is that once you've got a system, it becomes second nature. And yes, some models (like Fulfilled by Amazon) can even handle the shipping for you!

Keys to Profitability:

- Be consistent. Even listing two to three items a day adds up.
- Offer great customer service. People buy from people they trust.
- Focus on trending, high-demand items or unique finds that solve problems.

Real Talk:

E-commerce is the perfect bridge for anyone who's in transition. Whether you're rebuilding your finances, trying to leave a job, or simply wanting to *try something new*—it's a path paved with possibility. You don't need a fancy brand. You just need faith and follow-through.

When I made my first $100 on Facebook Marketplace, I didn't just see profit—I saw *proof*. Proof that God can use the small things to make a big difference. Proof that obedience in action creates overflow.

Affiliate Marketing & Influencer Partnerships

Sharing What You Love—and Getting Paid for It

This income stream was a game-changer for me. It felt like *finally* getting rewarded for the recommendations I was already making. I realized that I'd been sending people to Amazon, apps, and courses for years without ever getting a thank-you—until I discovered affiliate marketing.

As women, we *naturally* share what we love. Whether it's that Amazon gadget that made RV life easier or a journal that helped us stay grounded, our word carries influence. What if that influence became an income stream?

Affiliate marketing and influencer partnerships let you *monetize your authenticity*. When done right, it's not about selling—it's about serving your audience by curating helpful, high-value solutions that actually bless their life.

What It Is:

You earn commissions by promoting products, courses, or services created by other people or companies. Whether it's a beauty tool, a software subscription, or a trading app, every click and sale through your link can turn into passive income.

Why It Matters:

- It's low risk, high reward. No inventory. No shipping. No customer service.

- It honors your God-given voice and influence. Your story, your experience, your journey matters—and it can empower others while creating income.
- It's flexible and scalable. You can build once (a post, a video, a blog) and let it work for you over time.
- It helps you practice good stewardship—earning from the value you already add in everyday conversations.

I always say: if you're going to talk about it anyway, you might as well get paid for it.

Getting Started:

1. **Pick Your Partners:** Join affiliate programs that align with your values—Amazon, Canva, KDP, trading platforms, or any tool you *actually use and love.*
2. **Create Content with Heart:** Share a video, reel, blog, or post about *why* you love it and *how* it's helped you. Be real. That's what converts.
3. **Use Smart Links:** Add affiliate links to your bio, captions, blog, or emails. Use link tracking tools to see what's working.
4. **Repeat and Refine:** See what your audience responds to, then create more content that answers their questions and makes their life easier.

Time vs. Money:

This is one of the low-cost ways to get started. You don't need a product—you just need passion and consistency. Time is spent mostly on content creation and relationship-building, but over time, your old posts can keep generating income long after you hit "publish."

Keys to Profitability:

- Be authentic. People don't want a sales pitch—they want a trusted friend who's already tried it.
- Choose quality products. Promote what you genuinely believe in so your integrity stays intact.
- Create searchable content. Think: "What would *you* Google if you were trying to solve that problem?"

Real Talk:

Affiliate marketing is the ultimate blend of purpose and profit. You get to help people shortcut their search for what works—and get rewarded in the process.

For me, every affiliate check that comes in is a little *reminder* that obedience leads to overflow. That something I said, something I *shared...* helped someone take action, solve a problem, or feel seen. And that's ministry too.

So don't downplay your influence. When you share from a place of value, *everyone wins*—including you.

Digital Products & Publishing

Package Your Wisdom, Publish with Purpose

There's something sacred about taking what God has taught you and turning it into a tool that can bless someone else's life. That's exactly what digital products allow you to do. Whether it's an eBook, prayer journal, vision board planner, or a mini-course—you're not just selling content. You're impacting lives.

This is one of the most empowering income streams I've ever built. Why? Because it allows you to share your testimony, your expertise, or your creativity in a way that keeps giving over and over again.

If you've ever written out advice for a friend, created a checklist to organize your chaos, or recorded a voice note full of encouragement—guess what? You already have the *bones* of a digital product.

What It Is:

Digital products and publishing allow you to create once and sell repeatedly—with zero inventory and global reach. With tools like Amazon KDP, Canva, and simple course platforms, you can launch your journal, guide, or mini-course with no warehouse, no shipping labels, and no storefront—just purpose packaged into profit.

Why It Matters:

- This is legacy income. Once it's published, it can serve people long after you've hit "upload."
- You get to be the author of your story—literally and figuratively.
- It lets you scale impact without trading time for dollars.
- You'll be amazed at how God will use your obedience to reach strangers in places you've never even been.

For me, publishing *God is My Source* and *Crypto Key Keeper* wasn't just business—it was ministry. Every journal entry, every seed phrase page, every affirmation was written with the reader's breakthrough in mind.

Getting Started:

1. **Pick a Purposeful Topic:** What do people ask you about? What do you wish existed when *you* were starting out? Let that lead your first product.
2. **Create with Excellence:** Use Canva or BookBolt to design clean, professional interiors and covers. You don't need to be a designer—just stay consistent with your message and brand.

3. **Publish & Promote:** Amazon KDP is a great launchpad. Upload your file, set your price, and optimize with good keywords. Share your product on social, email, and with your community.

4. **Rinse & Repeat:** Once you've done one, the next one is easier. Build a library of products that walk alongside your reader's journey.

Time vs. Money:

Expect to invest upfront time developing your content and formatting—but once it's live, the ongoing maintenance is minimal. You can literally make sales in your sleep.

Keys to Profitability:

- Know your niche. Speak directly to a specific person with a specific problem.
- Present with polish. A beautiful cover and clean formatting go a long way.
- Market like a mentor. Show how your product helped *you* and how it can help *them* too.

Real Talk:

This is one of the most accessible and powerful income streams you can start—no warehouse, no staff, no excuses. Just your voice, your story, and your obedience.

Don't let fear of imperfection stop you. My first KDP journal wasn't perfect, but it was *published*. And it's still blessing people today.

So go ahead, sis—create the resource you wish *you* had. Package your breakthrough and put it into someone else's hands. That's not just income—that's impact.

Cash Flow Collective & Money Mindset Membership

A Sacred Space for Women to Heal, Grow, and Prosper Together

This isn't just a subscription. This is a **movement**. A safe, spirit-led space where faith-driven women link arms, renew their money mindsets, and take bold action toward financial freedom—with accountability, support, and coaching every step of the way.

When I created the *Cash Flow Collective*, it wasn't because I had it all figured out. It was because I knew how lonely this journey could feel—and I also knew the *power of community* when it's rooted in **faith, finances, and freedom**. If you've ever craved a sisterhood where you could **learn, unlearn, rebuild, and rise**, this was built for you.

What It Is:

This is a membership-based mentorship space where we focus on rewiring old money patterns, learning smart (and spirit-led) financial strategies, and supporting one another as we walk out our **God-given abundance**—all while building sustainable income streams.

Think:

- Monthly mindset coaching calls.
- Exact income streams I personally used to go from Broke and Broken to BornAgain Bo$$Babe.
- Guest trainings from experts.
- A supportive community for real conversations.
- Practical steps to steward and multiply your income, creating income streams that align with your lifestyle.

You'll get access to lessons I've learned through the fire—plus frameworks that helped me go from broke and burned out to **Bo$$Babe and blessed**.

Don't Know Where to Start?

If you're reading this and thinking, *"That sounds amazing, but I don't even know what my income stream could be yet..."* — let me personally invite you to join us inside the **Cash Flow Collective**.

This is exactly the space where clarity begins.

You don't need a finished product, fancy funnel, or 10,000 followers. You just need willingness.

Let us help you uncover your gifts, align with your calling, and explore options that fit your lifestyle, values, and purpose.

You don't have to build alone—we'll figure it out *together*.

Visit bornagainbossbabe.comor connect with me on Facebook to learn more and join the next cohort.

Ready to use your talents to start your own community?

Getting Started:

1. **Design Your Framework:** Create tiered membership levels that offer clear value—coaching, replays, mini-courses, or private chats.
2. **Choose Your Platform:** Whether it's Kajabi, Mighty Networks, Skool, or even a Facebook group with Stripe, the tech can be simple.
3. **Launch With Intention:** Start with a founding round— invite ten women who align with the mission and grow from there. Make it personal, not perfect.

4. **Lead With Love & Structure:** Schedule weekly calls, monthly themes, and Q&A sessions to help members actually *apply* what they're learning.

5. **Empower Others to Do the Same:** After walking your journey, pass the baton. Encourage others to create their own coaching circles, digital communities, or mastermind groups based on their unique gifts, experiences, and areas of wisdom.

Time vs. Money:

This stream does need **hands-on commitment**—showing up for your people, creating content, and staying present. But in exchange? You gain **predictable recurring revenue** and the joy of watching transformation happen in real-time.

Keys to Profitability:

- **High-value content.** Don't just inspire—equip. Give your members *tools*, not just talk.
- **Engaged community.** Make them feel seen, known, and safe.
- **Authentic leadership.** Your story is the bridge to their breakthrough—show up vulnerably and consistently.

Final Word:

This is your sign to **stop waiting for someone else** to create the space you wish existed.

God may be calling *you* to build it.

Whether you're just starting out or you're ready to lead your own membership or mastermind, know this: your lived experience has value.

Your story matters. And there are women out there *waiting* for you to show up, so they can rise too.

By serving up a variety of income "flavors," you protect yourself from unexpected shifts and create multiple pathways to freedom. Start with the flavor that calls to you most, then add another as your confidence—and your revenue—grows. Each stream illuminates a different facet of your God-given talents, turning your lemonade stand into a thriving business empire.

Marketing Your Stand—Branding, Content & Community

When you show up as **you**—bold, authentic, faith-filled—you create a brand that lasts, no matter which "flavors" you add or remove. Here's how you build that brand and cultivate a community that keeps coming back for more.

1. Tell Your Story with Faith at the Center

You aren't just selling products—you're sharing your journey. Start by crafting your founder's story: why you became a Born Again Bo$$Babe, how God carried you from broke to brave, and what lessons you've learned along the way. When you weave faith through those pivotal moments, your audience sees someone they can trust and root for.

2. Brand Yourself—Not Just Your Business

By branding **YOU**, you give yourself the freedom to add or remove "flavors" as your empire evolves. Your personal brand ensures you never have to start over when you pivot. I built **Tara Tried It** alongside my Born Again Bo$$Babe identity because people kept asking, "Have you tried this?" Positioning myself as the go-to tester for gadgets, services, and side hustles keeps me relevant—even when my menu changes. Decide on your signature look, voice, and values, and let them guide every new venture.

3. Master Your Social Media Recipe

- **Pick the Right Platforms:** Identify where your ideal customers spend time. Instagram for quick inspiration; Facebook and YouTube for deeper tutorials or live Q&As.
- **Define Content Pillars:** Choose three to five themes—like Faith & Finance, Lemonade Lessons, and Lifestyle Flexibility—and cycle through them, so your feed always feels fresh.
- **Be Consistent:** Follow a simple schedule: inspirational Reels on Mondays, tutorials on Wednesdays, and daily behind-the-scenes stories. Consistency builds trust and expectation.

4. Activate Networking & Referrals

Your network can become your most powerful marketing engine.

- **Accountability Pods:** Form small mastermind groups (three to five women) who meet monthly to share wins, troubleshoot challenges, and pray for one another.
- **Referral Rewards:** Offer special bonuses or discounts to customers who refer friends to your membership or products.
- **Cross-Promotions:** Collaborate with complementary Bo$$Babes for joint webinars or Instagram Lives—sharing audiences multiplies your reach.

5. Host Mini "Tastings"—Local & Online Events

Just like you'd sample lemonade before buying a glass, give your audience a taste of your expertise:

- **Webinars & Workshops:** Teach one powerful concept in 30 to 60 minutes, then invite attendees to take the next step in your program.

- **Live Q&A Sessions:** Schedule 15-minute sessions on Facebook or Instagram where you answer burning questions about faith, finance, or entrepreneurship.
- **Virtual Pop-Ups:** If you sell digital downloads, host a weekend event in your Facebook group or on your website where customers can grab special bundles at a discount.

By owning your story, investing in a flexible personal brand, and consistently engaging through content and community, you'll transform casual followers into raving fans—people who believe in you and support your pink lemonade stand every step of the way.

Automating the Process—Systems & Outsourcing

If you want to scale beyond "one-woman show," automation and smart delegation are non-negotiable. When you work **on** your business—building systems and processes—instead of **in** your business, you free up time to dream bigger and serve more people.

Active vs. Passive Income

- **Active Income:** Your time directly trades for money. Coaching calls, live webinars, and in-person sales.
- **Passive Income:** Set-and-forget streams that earn while you sleep—automated trading bots, digital products, and affiliate sales.

Aim for a healthy mix. Your **active** offerings keep cash flowing and relationships strong, while **passive** streams build residual revenue and buy back your time.

Lean Systems: Build Once, Benefit Forever

- **Email Funnels:** Use Mailchimp or ConvertKit to automatically welcome new subscribers, nurture trust, and promote your offers.
- **Scheduling Tools:** Tools like Calendly or Acuity let clients book calls without the back-and-forth. Block out "deep work" times to protect focus.
- **Analytics Dashboards:** Track key metrics—open rates, clicks, conversions—with Google Analytics or platform insights to know what's working.

Outsourcing: Delegate What Isn't Your Zone of Genius

Your network is more than a support group—it's a resource bank. Before you look on Upwork or Fiverr, ask within your community:

- **Fellow Entrepreneurs:** Who excels at graphic design, copywriting, or website development?
- **Past Colleagues:** Who has accounting or bookkeeping skills you can tap for monthly finances?
- **Faith-Based Groups:** Who has event-planning or social-media expertise?

By leveraging people you already trust, you maintain quality and share opportunities within your circle. Then fill any remaining gaps with:

- **Virtual Assistants (VAs):** Hire VAs for routine tasks—email management, social scheduling, and customer support.
- **Specialized Freelancers:** Find designers, editors, or ad specialists on freelancer sites for project-based work.
- **Boutique Agencies:** Partner for complex needs like paid ads or SEO, ensuring professional results as you scale.

Implement Systems Quickly with a PinkPrint Mindset

When systems feel overwhelming, lean on your **Action Over Analysis** approach:

1. **Mindset Reset:** Pray for clarity, remind yourself that "done is better than perfect."
2. **Ready, Set, Go:** Sketch a simple workflow in a Google Doc or on a whiteboard.
3. **Delegate Immediately:** Identify what you must do and what your network or hires can handle—then hand it off.

You built your lemonade stand to serve customers, not drown in busywork. By automating key processes and outsourcing tasks—especially to talented people in your own network—you reclaim your most precious commodity: time. Now you can pour your energy into vision, strategy, and the next big flavor you're ready to serve.

Pricing for Profit and Purpose

Perfecting your recipe isn't enough—you must price it so you can thrive and give back. Your rates should reflect the value you deliver, honor God with your first fruits, and sustain your stand for the long haul.

Value-Based Pricing: Charge What You're Worth

Don't undercut yourself out of fear. Value-based pricing asks: **What transformation does your pink lemonade provide?** If you're coaching women to launch new income streams, your hourly rate should match not just your time, but the freedom and confidence you deliver.

- **Assess Impact:** Calculate the dollar—or life—value of your results (e.g., a client who earns an extra $5,000 using your system).

- **Communicate Benefits:** In your sales page and discovery calls, focus on outcomes ("By working together, you'll..."), not just features.
- **Test & Adjust:** Start with a confident rate, gather feedback, and raise your prices as demand grows.

Tithing & Reinvestment: First Fruits in Business

Malachi 3:10 (NIV) reminds us to "Bring the whole tithe into the storehouse, that there may be food in my house. Test Me in this and see if I will not throw open the floodgates of heaven and pour out so much blessing that there will not be room enough to store it." In business, that means giving God the first portion of every profit.

- **Tithe Your Revenue:** Commit 10 percent of your gross income to your local church or Kingdom work before covering expenses.
- **Reinvest Wisely:** Allocate another percentage—say 10 to 20 percent—to tools, education, or team members who help you scale.
- **Watch Provision Multiply:** When you honor God first, He honors you with creativity, connections, and financial increase.

Profit Margins: Track Costs vs. Revenue

Knowing your numbers keeps your stand sustainable. Profit margin is simply: **(Revenue – Costs) ÷ Revenue**. Aim for at least a 50 percent margin on digital products and 20 to 30 percent on physical goods or services.

- **List All Costs:** Include direct costs (inventory, software subscriptions) and indirect costs (marketing ads, subcontractor fees).
- **Review Monthly:** Use a simple spreadsheet or accounting software to compare revenue against expenses each month.

- **Adjust as Needed:** If margins dip, raise prices, reduce costs, or refine your offering to maintain healthy growth.

When you price with purpose—charging for value, tithing first, and tracking profits—you build a thriving, sustainable business that blesses you, your customers, and the Kingdom. Your lemonade stand isn't just a side hustle; it's a fruitful enterprise grounded in faith and financial stewardship.

Managing Your Time—Work Around Your Life

No matter how many "flavors" you're serving, your success depends on one non-renewable resource: **time.** To build your empire without sacrificing what matters most—family, faith, and self-care—you must learn to work **around** your life, not let your business dictate it. Here's how to create a schedule that honors both your goals and your well-being.

Time Blocking: PinkPrint Scheduling for Busy Women

Time blocking turns a chaotic day into a clear roadmap. Instead of reacting to every email and request, you carve out dedicated slots for your highest priorities.

1. **Identify Your Core Pillars:** Faith, family, business, self-care.
2. **Assign Blocks:** Reserve morning hours for prayer and planning, midday for deep work, afternoons for family or outreach, and evenings for rest or reflection.
3. **Protect Your Blocks:** Treat each block like a meeting with God or your most important client—no distractions allowed.

By visually mapping your week, you say **yes** to what you value and **no** to everything else.

Batching & Focused Days: Efficiency in Every Task

Group similar tasks together to maximize focus and flow.

- **Batch Content Creation:** Write all blog posts or record videos for the week in one session.
- **Batch Admin Work:** Set aside one afternoon for emails, invoicing, and scheduling.
- **Theme Your Days:** Make Mondays "Marketing Mondays," Tuesdays "Training Tuesdays," etc.

When you minimize context-switching, you gain momentum and finish more in less time—freeing up space for what truly matters.

Work–Life Blend: Balance Without Burnout

Work-life "balance" doesn't mean equal hours; it means intentional choices about how you spend your time. Every **yes** you give to work is a **no** to something else—so choose wisely.

- **Grind with Purpose:** When a launch or deadline demands extra hours, lean in wholeheartedly—but set an end date.
- **Prioritize Family Moments:** Guard special times—Sunday dinners, bedtime stories, date nights—as non-negotiable blocks on your calendar.
- **Integrate Faith & Rest:** Schedule a weekly Sabbath or spiritual retreat—time to recharge your soul.

Remember, unrelenting achievement shines brightest when your life is well-lived. By aligning your schedule with your faith and values, you nurture the whole you—mind, body, and spirit—and maintain the stamina to seize every opportunity.

Balance isn't a destination; it's a daily practice of saying **yes** to what matters and **no** to what distracts. When you honor your entire self—family, faith, and business—you become not just a successful entrepreneur, but a flourishing woman who inspires others to live their best lives, too.

Scaling Up—From Stand to Franchise

You've perfected your recipe, automated your processes, and built a loyal following. Now, it's time to grow—from a one-woman stand into a thriving franchise of pink lemonade offerings. Scaling isn't about doing more yourself; it's about empowering others, expanding your reach, and upholding the values that made you irresistible in the first place.

Knowing When to Hire Your First Team Member

You'll know you're ready when you...

- Spend more time on administrative tasks than on high-impact strategy.
- Feel stretched thin and worry that clients or quality are slipping through the cracks.
- Have a steady demand you can't meet alone without burning out.

Bring on a **virtual assistant** or **part-time team member** to handle routine tasks—email triage, calendar management, order processing—so you can focus on vision, leadership, and the next big flavor.

Expanding into New "Locations"

Just as a lemonade franchise stretches from one corner of town to another, extend your brand across platforms and markets:

- **Platforms:** Launch on TikTok, LinkedIn, or podcast networks to reach fresh audiences.

- **Markets:** Adapt offerings for corporate wellness programs, church retreats, or college workshops.

Research each new "location," pray for guidance, and tailor your recipe to local tastes.

Adding New "Flavors" Based on Customer Feedback

Your community holds the best insights. When clients rave about your mindset mini-course, consider a deep-dive masterclass. If they request bite-sized tips, launch a weekly "lemonade shot" email series. Each new flavor must align with your PinkPrint values—faith, freedom, and female empowerment—to keep growth authentic.

Building Your Affiliate Army

Don't just hire employees—recruit an **affiliate army** to build your business alongside you.

- **Identify Superfans:** Those who already love your offerings and share their success stories.
- **Provide Tools:** Give affiliates swipe-files, graphics, and email templates so they can promote seamlessly.
- **Offer Competitive Commissions:** Reward every referral or sale they generate.
- **Regular Training & Recognition:** Host quarterly calls, share top-performer spotlights, and celebrate wins to keep motivation high.

An engaged affiliate network multiplies your reach, bringing new customers to your stand while you focus on next-level strategy.

Maintaining Quality & PinkPrint Values as You Grow

Growth can tempt you to cut corners. Guard your values by:

- **Standard Operating Procedures (SOPs):** Document every process—onboarding members, shipping products, hosting webinars—so every team member and affiliate delivers the same exceptional experience.

- **Regular Team & Affiliate Check-Ins:** Schedule monthly meetings or a private community space to realign on mission, share wins, and troubleshoot hurdles.
- **Cultivate a Culture of Faith & Excellence:** Infuse your company and affiliate community with prayer, gratitude, and a commitment to serve. When every partner embodies PinkPrint principles, customers feel the difference.

Scaling is as much a faith journey as a business strategy. As you welcome team members, step into new markets, craft fresh offerings, and build your affiliate army, trust that God guides every expansion. Your stand is no longer just a solo venture—it's a franchise of faith-filled impact, spreading sweet lemonade lessons across every corner of your world.

Faith & Finances—Stewarding Your Stand

Your business isn't just a revenue engine—it's a ministry. The Holy Spirit is your most powerful mentor and ally, guiding every decision, big or small. When you keep God at the center of your finances, you'll always taste the sweetest outcomes.

Keep God at the Center of Every Revenue Decision

Before you set a price, launch a new product, or sign a contract, pause and pray. Ask the Holy Spirit to illuminate your next step:

- **"Lord, is this aligned with Your purpose for me?"**
- **"Will this honor You and serve my customers well?"**

By inviting God into your boardroom, you tap into divine wisdom that outperforms any market forecast.

Honor Him with Your Profits through Generosity & Tithing

Malachi 3:10 challenges us to bring our "first fruits" to the storehouse. In business, that means:

1. **Tithe Your Revenue:** Commit 10 percent of every sale or paycheck to Kingdom work through your church or a ministry you trust.
2. **Give Beyond the Tithe:** Allocate a portion of profits to charitable causes, affiliate bonuses, or helping a sister-in-business get started.

Generosity isn't just a nice gesture—it's a spiritual strategy that unlocks God's abundance.

Trust His Provision as You Scale

As you expand into new markets and add flavors to your menu, you may face moments of uncertainty. Remember:

- **God Owns the Store:** He's the ultimate Provider—every customer, every idea, every resource originates with Him.
- **Lean Into His Promises:** Pray Malachi 3:10 over your finances, claiming His promise of abundance.
- **Celebrate His Faithfulness:** Keep a financial "blessing log" to record unexpected revenues, timely referrals, and providential partnerships.

When you steward your stand in partnership with the Holy Spirit—praying over numbers, tithing first, and trusting His daily provision—you build not only a profitable empire but a legacy that glorifies God. Your stand becomes more than a business; it becomes a beacon of His faithfulness and generosity in your world.

Turning Your Ideas into Income

You've learned how to mix your signature recipe, set up a stand that's built to last, and serve multiple flavors that generate both active and passive income. You've seen the power of branding yourself, automating key processes, building an affiliate army, and scaling with integrity and faith. Most importantly, you've discovered how keeping God at the center of every decision turns your business into a ministry—one that blesses you, your customers, and the Kingdom.

Use this chapter as your step-by-step recipe guide. Mix your unique ingredients, serve your market with excellence, and watch God multiply your efforts into lasting financial and time freedom.

Reflection Questions

- Which "flavor" of income most excites you, and what's one step you can take this week to start it?
- How can you apply a PinkPrint mindset reset when fear or perfectionism slows your launch?
- Who will you recruit into your accountability circle to keep you on track?
- What systems can you automate or outsource this month to free up more of your time?
- How will you honor God with your first profits?

CHAPTER 7

The Hero in You — Becoming Your Own Bo$$Babe

Congratulations, Beautiful Bo$$Babe—You Made It.

You've arrived at the final chapter of the PinkPrint journey, and this moment deserves a celebration. Not just for reaching the end of a book—but for every step you've taken, every obstacle you've faced, and every sour moment you've transformed into something sweet.

This chapter is where I pause to reflect—not just on the words written here, but on the path I've walked: from a little girl learning resilience and responsibility to the Born Again Bo$$Babe I am today. And it's where I invite you to rise into your own story, your own PinkPrint, your own power.

Here, we're going to redefine what success looks like—on your terms, not by the world's standards, but by the three pillars that bring lasting meaning: **Faith**, **Freedom**, and **Financial Growth.**

I'll share how God's hand has guided me through every pivot, how deep-rooted relationships became my anchors, and how building multiple income streams gave me the flexibility to design a life I truly love.

But don't think of this as the end. This chapter isn't a period—it's your launching pad. A sacred space where we celebrate your transformation from the girl squeezing lemons to the woman confidently serving up her own signature batch of pink lemonade. This is your moment to own your PinkPrint—blending mindset shifts, faith-fueled habits, practical strategies, and powerful community into a roadmap for your next level.

As you step into your full identity as a Born Again Bo$$Babe, remember: your greatest chapter isn't behind you. It's being written right now—one faithful, fearless, fabulous step at a time.

Where I Am Now

As I pause to reflect on where I am today, one word rises above all: gratitude. This PinkPrint journey hasn't just changed my circumstances—it has transformed my mindset, deepened my faith, and aligned my mission with God's greater plan.

Faith is the heartbeat behind every decision I make. My husband and I are blessed to be part of a thriving, spirit-filled church that continually fuels our walk with God. Between weekly services, small groups, and soul-nourishing conversations at home, I stay anchored through intentional prayer, journaling, and listening to the whispers of the Holy Spirit. I've learned that divine direction always shows up—on God's timeline, with clarity, peace, and purpose.

Family time—especially with my husband—is one of the deepest joys of my life. Whether we're traveling together, relaxing on the couch, or diving into a new business or crypto project, these sacred moments are the legacy we're building together. Prioritizing my marriage means protecting our time and creating space for dreams, connection, and laughter. This partnership isn't just love—it's purpose in motion.

Multiple income streams have given me something priceless: options. Most mornings begin with gold trading before the sun even rises. I co-lead empowering trading calls with my friend Sarah, where we pour into our community with strategy, mindset coaching, and comedy to keep it fun. By 10:00 a.m., I shift gears—writing new KDP journals, creating affiliate content, mentoring inside the Cash Flow Collective, and mapping out new revenue ideas. Each "flavor" of income was intentionally built to reflect my gifts and values. Together, they support the life I once could only envision in prayer.

Time freedom is the ultimate flex. Whether it's spontaneous coffee dates with fellow Bo$$Babes, afternoon coaching calls, or quiet walks where I talk to God about what's next, I've created a life that allows me to say "yes" to what truly matters. This isn't just success—it's alignment.

My Pink Lemonade Moment: Just the other day, I wrapped up profitable morning trades, drove to Tampa for a business expo, had a power lunch with the CEO of a company I'm affiliated with, and came home to dinner with my husband, where we dreamed up our next big adventure. In the middle of it all, I paused, smiled, and whispered, "Thank you, God." Because this life—this rhythm of grace, growth, and gratitude—is exactly what I prayed for in the valleys, and now, I'm living in the overflow.

Redefining Success

Let's talk about *real* success—not the Instagram highlight reels or the six-figure screenshots, but the kind of success that actually fills your soul.

For the longest time, I thought success was just about numbers—income goals, follower counts, and crossing items off my vision board. But life, faith, and a few detours taught me that *net worth* means nothing if your *self-worth* is bankrupt. True abundance can't be measured in dollars alone. It's found in peace, purpose, and alignment.

Success, for me now, is a life where **faith, freedom, and finances flow together**.

- Faith keeps me grounded, reminding me that God is my ultimate provider and strategist.
- Freedom allows me to say *yes* to what matters and *no* to what doesn't—whether that's time with my husband, prayer walks, or spontaneous business adventures.
- Finances give me options. Not just to live comfortably, but to *give generously*, *create fearlessly*, and *serve joyfully*.

These three pillars—Faith, Freedom, and Finance—aren't separate lanes. They're woven together like a braid, each one strengthening the other. And when they're aligned, your life becomes an overflow of impact and joy.

One of my favorite quotes says:

> **"A hero is an ordinary individual
> who perseveres despite obstacles."**

And let me tell you: *you don't need a cape, a title, or permission to become the hero of your own story.* What you need is a resilient heart, a willing spirit, and the courage to keep going when life tries to knock you down.

You've already proven that you're still standing. Now, it's time to define what you're standing *for*.

Success Snapshot Exercise:

Take a moment to write your new definition of success in one sentence.
Not what the world says. Not what your past says.
But what your *faith-filled future self* declares.

"Success for me is..."

Let it be your new anchor. Write it down. Tape it to your mirror. Pray over it. Speak it until it becomes your reality.

Applying Your PinkPrint

Now that you've seen the power of the PinkPrint in action, it's time to make it personal. Your PinkPrint isn't just a theory—it's your action plan, your roadmap, your invitation to transformation.

Let's revisit the five foundational steps we've covered in this journey:

- **Mindset Reset:** Rewire your thoughts and speak life over your future. What you believe is what you build.
- **Faith Over Fear:** When fear whispers "What if?", faith responds "Even if." You don't need to have it all figured out— just trust the One who does.
- **Dream Big & Goal Small**: Your God-sized vision is valid, but it comes to life through small, daily, obedient steps.
- **Network Power:** You don't have to do this alone. Surround yourself with people who water your vision, not wither it.

- **Action Over Analysis**: Progress beats perfection every time. God can't bless what you're not willing to move on from.

Your Personal PinkPrint Roadmap

Now, it's your turn to implement. Here's how to put your PinkPrint into motion this week:

Commit to One Mindset Tool
Whether it's journaling, affirmations, or rewriting limiting beliefs—choose one and use it consistently.

Choose a Faith Practice
Begin each morning with prayer, read scripture that speaks into your purpose, or designate quiet time each week to reflect and recharge.

Outline One Big Dream and Three Small Goals
For example, your big dream might be launching a digital product store. Three small goals could include: 1) defining your niche, 2) choosing your platform, 3) uploading your first product.

Identify Your Accountability Partner
Find someone who will lovingly call you higher and keep you aligned. Share your goals and invite regular check-ins.

Schedule Your Next Step (Even if Imperfect)
Pick a date. Add it to your calendar. Take the step. You don't need perfection to create momentum—just action.

Real-Life Example: Meet Jeanny

Jeanny and her husband had a dream to live aboard a boat and turn it into a charter dinner cruise venue to help fund their lifestyle. Here's how she applied the PinkPrint:

- **Mindset Reset**: She began her mornings declaring, "I am equipped, empowered, and positioned to prosper."
- **Faith Over Fear**: She prayed over their finances and trusted God to provide the resources and connections they needed.
- **Dream Big & Goal Small**: The big vision was to launch a flexible, purpose-driven business from their boat. She broke it down into simple steps: partner with a local restaurant with a dock, market on social media, and host a test cruise for friends.
- **Network Power**: She connected with other entrepreneurs and leaned into a supportive circle that provided encouragement and practical advice.
- **Action Over Analysis**: Instead of waiting until everything was perfect, she launched M/Y Firefly Cruises with one short video and a basic website: **ancloterivertours.com**

People showed up. Her community grew. And her confidence blossomed—not because everything was perfect, but because she took action, trusted God, and simply got started.

You don't need a million followers. You need one obedient step.

You don't need certainty. You need clarity of calling.

And most of all, you need to trust that the PinkPrint already lives within you.

Embracing Your Unstoppable Potential

This is the moment where you stop shrinking back and start standing tall in your story. Everything you've walked through—every detour, delay, and disappointment—was preparing you for the powerhouse you're becoming. Your setbacks weren't signs to stop; they were setups to pivot.

Own Your Story

The world doesn't need perfection—it needs your authenticity. The chapters you once wanted to skip are often the very ones God uses to set others free. When you embrace your journey, with all its twists and turns, you give other women permission to do the same. You're not broken—you're battle-tested.

Celebrate Small Wins

Too often, we rush to the next milestone, forgetting to honor what we've already accomplished. But progress, no matter how small, is still progress. Start a weekly gratitude list. Celebrate when you post your first product. Acknowledge when you hit a savings goal. Thank God for the doors He's opened and the ones He closed to protect you. Joy is found in the journey, not just the destination.

Lean Into Community

God didn't design you to build your empire alone. The people around you matter. Keep growing your affiliate team and mastermind pods. Collaborate, communicate, and stay accountable. When one woman rises, she lifts others with her. Find your faith-filled tribe—and be a light in theirs, too.

Next-Level Faith

Now is the time to stretch your prayers and your vision. Ask God for boldness to pursue the big, scary dreams He's placed in your heart. The ones that make you question, "Can I really do this?" That's usually where His glory shows up the most. You don't have to know how—it's not your job to know how. It's your job to believe and take the next step. Remember: God specializes in the impossible.

Action Prompt:

Write a Letter to Your Future Bo$$Babe Self.

Tell her what you're building, how you're believing, and what you promise never to give up on. Seal it, date it, and set a reminder to read it one year from now.

I've personally done this exercise at an entrepreneurial conference where we were asked to write our dream life down on paper. They mailed our letters back to us a year later—and I was amazed to realize that over 80 percent of what I had written had either come true or was actively in motion. There is power in writing down your goals and dreams. Let your own words become proof that your faith has action behind it.

And always remember:

What tries to stop you only fuels you.
You are not here by accident.
You are not average.
You are not disqualified.

You are a Born Again Bo$$Babe. And this world hasn't seen anything yet.

Reflection Questions

Take a few moments to pause, breathe, and reflect on your journey so far. Let these questions guide you into deeper clarity and purpose:

- What does success look like now—in faith, family, freedom, and finance?
- Which PinkPrint step transformed you the most, and how can you build on it?
- What's one *imperfect* action you can take today toward your next big dream?
- Who will cheer you on when obstacles arise—and how will you stay connected?
- How will you celebrate the hero within you this week?

Your Pink Pitcher Awaits

As you close this book, I want you to know: the same God who carried you through every breakdown and breakthrough is the One who poured your unique PinkPrint into your heart. You've always had the recipe within you. Now, your "pitcher" of dreams, talents, and purpose stands ready—just waiting for you to pour in faith, courage, and action.

You don't need to wait for perfect timing. You don't need to have it all figured out.

You just need to **start pouring.**

A Blessing for Your Journey:

May your life overflow with the sweet taste of victory, the refreshing joy of time well spent with loved ones, and the abundant provision that comes when you faithfully steward every gift God has placed in your hands.

May your days be filled with purpose, your steps guided by peace, and your hustle always anchored in Heaven's grace.

Go forth as the hero God designed you to be—bold, brilliant, and built for impact.

Pour your pink lemonade into a world thirsty for hope.

Step up to your stand, mix your next batch, and let your God-given flavors shine. The world needs your pink lemonade now.

**Congratulations, Bo$$Babe—
your greatest chapter is just beginning!**

Now, go live it.

About the Author

Tara Hirshberg is a serial entrepreneur, trading mentor, content creator, and faith-filled freedom coach who turned her rock-bottom moment into a multi-stream income empire. Known as the "Born Again Bo$$Babe," Tara empowers women to create flexible, purpose-led businesses that align with faith, family, and financial freedom. When she's not mentoring women through side hustles, trading, or passive income streams, she's traveling the country in her RV—living proof that lemonade can be made anywhere. Learn more at BornAgainBossBabe.com

Your PinkPrint Starts Now

When life handed me lemons, I made *pink lemonade*—and built an empire with it.

In these pages, you've witnessed my journey from broke and broken to born again and booming. I didn't write this book from a mountaintop—I wrote it from the messy middle, with tear-stained journal pages, unanswered prayers, and a faith that wouldn't quit.

If you're holding this book, you've already felt the tug.
You know you're meant for more.
You're craving purpose, flexibility, and the confidence to take bold steps toward your God-given calling.
You've outgrown survival mode—and you're ready for *strategy*.

Friend, this is your invitation to stop sitting on your potential and start walking in your PinkPrint—a proven, spirit-led system for building income streams that align with your purpose, passion, and priorities.

What Happens Next!

I didn't just write a book—I built a movement.

And I want *you* to be part of it.

At **BornAgainBossBabe.com**, you'll find everything I've created to help women just like you:

- **Plug-and-play income streams** you can launch from anywhere (even in your PJs)

- **Guided resources** to help you start your own journal, course, or digital product
- **Trading education** to help you earn while you learn—no jargon, just results
- **Affiliate-ready businesses** you can promote with mentorship included
- A **faith-fueled sisterhood** that reminds you: you don't have to do this alone

Let's Link Arms

"God doesn't call the qualified. He qualifies the called."

If you're willing, He's able—and I'm here to walk beside you.

Whether you're ready to join my **Cash Flow Collective**, tap into affiliate opportunities, or simply want to learn a new skill that no one can ever take from you—**your journey starts now.**

Visit BornAgainBossBabe.com
Get your free "JumpStart Challenge" starter guide + video series
Sign up for my newsletter and stay connected
Apply to become an **official Born Again Bo$$Babe Affiliate**

You've Got This

Your story isn't over. It's just getting good.
So take that first step. Turn the page of your life and build your own *PinkPrint to Perseverance.*
Let's create freedom, faith, and financial flow—*together.*